Creative Markdown Practices for Profit

Other Publications by Murray Krieger

637 EXCITING CAREERS IN FASHION AND
   MERCHANDISING

MERCHANDISING MATH FOR PROFIT

MERCHANDISING PLANBOOK AND SALES PROMOTION
   CALENDAR

PROFESSIONAL MANAGEMENT SERIES
   Dictionary of Buying and Merchandising
   Fundamentals of Buying and Merchandising
   Problems in Buying and Merchandising

DECISION-MAKING IN RETAILING AND MARKETING

ASSIGNMENT PROJECT WORKBOOK

MATHEMATICS OF RETAIL MERCHANDISING:
   THEORY AND PRACTICE

Creative Markdown Practices for Profit

Murray Krieger

Fairchild Publications, Inc.

NEW YORK

Contents

Preface

All things being equal, the essential elements for a successful operation are the retailer's ability to control expenses and shortages and the extent of the professionalism applied to the intelligent and skillful use of markdowns. Of the three elements, only markdowns are under the complete control of one person, the buyer.

A markdown is generally thought to be a device to dispose of old stock, slow-selling stock, or odds and ends. Other retailers use it to release needed capital tied up in dead stock. But many retailers have learned how to merchandise the markdown for profit and still achieve the objectives of cleaner stocks without freezing the capital. The old concept that the main purpose of the markdown was to correct buying mistakes has been replaced by more imaginative and innovative understandings of the scientific use of the markdown for additional profit.

This book has been written to provide interested merchandisers with the professionalism that can be gained through new understanding, changed attitudes, and increased abilities. The material has been prepared and presented to enable the beginning merchandiser to develop the needed skills in the planning, use, and control of the markdown as a positive tool for profit. For the veteran merchandiser, the information will serve to recharge the battery of experience. For the student, the presentation will provide new insights and an organized approach to the science of merchandising.

MURRAY KRIEGER

November, 1970

Introduction

When retailing was in its infancy, store owners were in daily contact with their merchandise and customers. The proprietor knew exactly what was selling, how fast and how much he could charge for it.

Pricing of merchandise was established by the desirability of the item, the neighborhood in which the store was located, overhead, and ultimate profit.

It was relatively simple to decide what one should be paying for the item and what one could hope to receive when selling it.

Seasons for soft goods were clearly noted four times a year and clearances were run at the end of each season to clean out old stock. Shrinkage and deterioration were minimal. Retailing was an emotional enterprise and buying and selling were predicated on personal taste and service.

The dynamic nature of retailing has been well demonstrated in the past fifty years. With the enormous growth of business, absentee ownership became prominent and significant changes had to take place in the operating policies and methods of retail stores.

Most justifiably, retailing has attained the status of a profession and as such has learned to employ the latest scientific aids in the distribution of merchandise to the consumer.

With the incredible growth of business, huge retail complexes, mass merchandising, discounting, and chain operations became the mode of the day.

The small store owner, in order to compete, had to learn to merchandise his operation in a scientific rather than haphazard manner.

The subject of markdowns is no longer a scholarly theme to be pursued by students. The knowledge of markdowns is the key to retail survival.

How to judge a markup is a well-known and practiced theory. Cost + overhead + profit + markdown = markup.

The importance of markdown has been sorely neglected and yet it is the markdown which is the lifeblood of the retail business.

To know when to take—how much of a reduction and for what purpose—can spell the difference between profit and loss.

Markdowns are caused by a variety of reasons, poor timing, wrong selection, wrong quantity, damages, deterioration, and change of season.

Markdowns are taken to stimulate sales, clear stock, develop open-to-buy, and increase traffic.

Markdowns result in realistic inventory counts, stimulation of interest among salespersons and consumers, and profit.

The key to a successful operation is the knowledge of markdowns in relation to timing and profits.

The built-in obsolescence of today's products, and the stimulus of advertising which makes impulse buying a specific pattern, necessitates the rapid turnover of all inventories. That is the first commandment of good business. Markdowns stimulate turnover and affect business much as proper medication affects good health.

I could think of no more important book for all students, merchandisers, and store owners than a volume devoted to the subject of markdowns.

ARTHUR BRESSMAN, VICE PRESIDENT

GENERAL MERCHANDISING MANAGER

Korvettes, A Division of Spartans Industries, Inc.

The more extensive a man's
knowledge of what has been
done, the greater will be
his power of knowing what
to do.

—DISRAELI

Creative Markdown Practices for Profit

[1] The Markdown Problem

Alexander Pope said, "Be not the first by whom the new are tried. Nor yet the last to lay the old aside." Many retailers would not agree with the first part of his thought, since the excitement in retailing comes from the newness, originality, creativity, and innovations provided by the leaders. But there are retailers who are not the first with the newest. These are the followers.

Probably, however, all retailers would give their assent to the latter part of the quote. There is no telling how many dollars in markdowns could have been prevented if only the buyer had taken the markdown when necessary. When the consumer has voted "no" on an item, no amount of rituals, prayers, candles, or good-luck charms will move the merchandise at the regular price. If every sincere effort has been made—through extra exposure of the merchandise and through the employment of extra selling, and merchandising techniques—and the merchandise still finds no acceptance, then it is time to apply the old adage, "Talk is cheap, but action is like gold from the hills." The action is the decision to take the markdown, quickly and effectively, to get ready cash to buy new, fresh merchandise.

A retailer once labeled a markdown as "a monument to misjudgment." While the misjudgment may be attributed to poor buying skill and to a lack of understanding of consumer wants and needs, one can find justification for some misjudgment in the words of Sidney L. Solomon: "By the very nature of retailing . . . obsolescence is inevitable in a dynamic industrial age; and human error will always prevail in the selection of styles, colors, and sizes ir correct quantities and assortments; furthermore, the plans of competition and the steps that must be taken to meet them are unpredictable." The misjudgment can be charged to the buyer, however, when he fails to develop skills in the use of the markdown as an effective tool for profit.

It has been said with reference to markdowns that "the first loss is the best loss," or "the first markdown is the cheapest markdown." Some retailers and store buyers find it difficult to understand this fundamental principle: that "dead" merchandise freezes the investment in the merchandise, thereby reducing available money for needed items. Out-of-date inventory at original prices depresses selling enthusiasm and discourages customer visits.

The fact remains that a markdown taken early enough, while the item is still in its selling season, will prevent both a larger markdown later and the diminished opportunities for sale that delayed markdowns cause. The words of Omar Khayyám, "Live for today, tomorrow may never come," can be paraphrased to read, "Take the markdown today, tomorrow may be too late."

The markdown problem in relation to buyers and retailers is the result of the many weaknesses of those involved in merchandising. The buyer delays taking the markdown because he regards it as evidence of a merchandising weakness. By taking the markdown, he is fearful that this weakness will be apparent and his lack of professionalism will thereby be revealed. Therefore, the markdown is delayed and the malignancy aggravated.

One of the major weaknesses leading to markdowns is an incorrect buying attitude, that of being product-oriented instead of consumer-oriented. Too many buyers depend upon the information supplied by the vendor for their buying decisions. The vendor informs him that Store XYZ has just ordered Style 672 and that Store ABC has bought Style 816, whereupon, by the process of irrational rationale, the buyer agrees to the purchase of styles 672 and 816. In essence, the buyer becomes a selling agent for the manufacturer instead of a purchasing agent for his consumers. If the purchased styles should happen to check out, the buyer's dependence on the vendor becomes more intense and his own skills less developed. If the styles should fail to check out, however, the weakness begins to compound itself in many different directions. Vendors deliver when they please, as they please, and what they please. It is no wonder that alert retailers are seriously making vendor-analysis studies to determine those vendors who are causing the greatest markdowns with the lowest profit return. The buyer's ineptness creates the problems that make it necessary for management to devote time, effort, and money later to discover the causes for the poor results.

Another weakness is the result of the buyer's lack of understanding and knowledge of the relationship between the markdown and the initial mark-on; the maintained mark-on; the cumulative mark-on; the open-to-buy; the gross margin; and the retail value of inventory method. How many merchandise personnel really have a working knowledge of the retail method of inventory? How many merchandise personnel are convinced that an additional markup offsets a markdown? It is this kind of naïveté that creates markdowns and subsequent problems.

A major weakness of some buyers is their lack of enthusiasm for the items they buy and their failure to transfer real enthusiasm to the selling personnel. Merchandise quietly finds its way into stock; it is not brought to the attention of the salespeople, and its potential excitement as a sales item is not communicated to the staff. A merchandise manager once said, "Enthusiasm is like the measles. It's catching." Smart buyers justify their purchases to the staff at meetings, or on an individual basis, because they have learned the value of making the salesperson a part of the buying and selling process. The buyer who makes the fatal mistake of telling his staff, "I bought the item although I'm not wild about it," virtually gives the item the kiss of death. The item's place on the markdown table is assured.

Such buyers would do well to heed the words of the late Bernard F. Gimbel, who told his buyers, "If you're only 99 percent sure, don't buy it!" The renowned Walter Hoving once said, "If it doesn't send a tingle up and down your spine, then it's not for you."

Sales people must be taught to know their merchandise. They might as well be ignorant of the English language as not to be able to give an intelligent reply about the goods they sell. But sales people are not mind readers, and must be taught. Yet how few stores, or their buyers, ever take time to explain the goods to the people that must sell them. Every buyer should fix stated times when he will demonstrate to his people the use, the value, the construction, the quality, and the comparative value of everything in stock so that exactly the arguments that sold him the goods may enable his people to sell them to the public. This will make goods sell twice as quickly, and with infinitely greater satisfaction to the customers.[1]

Would the reader believe that this statement was written in 1919 by W. R. Hotchkin, who was then sales manager for John Wanamaker in New York? Apparently the problem is a fundamental one that has and will continue to affect the profit of a retail operation.

A lack of communication and rapport between a buyer and the merchandise manager can lead to personal resentment on the part of the buyer. At a recent merchandising seminar, a merchandise manager stated that when he had made the mistake of buying an item abroad for one of his buyers without the buyer's knowledge, he found the item on two successive markdown sheets, the second a cut deeper than the first. He thought he'd see what was being done to move the merchandise—and found the entire stock in the drawer.

Probably the facet of the buyer's personality that most affects his buying decisions is a lack of a good taste level. A buyer with a low taste level who has no appreciation for, or understanding of, better merchandise is not able to relate either to his merchandise or to the consumers' needs. Conversely, a buyer with a high taste level who operates in the low-end price lines may feel built-in distaste for the merchandise. In either case, the approach to the buying decision may be tainted by the buyer's inability to relate the taste level to the ultimate satisfaction of the consumer.

One store executive said, "In the final analysis, all mark-

[1] W. R. Hotchkin, *The Manual of Successful Store Keeping* (New York: Doubleday, Page & Co., 1919), p. 176.

downs may be traced back to these fundamental errors—poor buying, poor selling." The key word is *poor*, for a lack of professionalism in the selection of merchandise affects the sales as well as the profits of every store. However, to knowledgeable buyers and merchandisers, a markdown is not an unconscionable evil but rather a potent force to be manipulated for the purpose of disposing of unwanted merchandise, and for assisting in the sale of merchandise. Dead stock ties up capital and kills profits, but this same dead stock can be made to work for the retailer to build traffic and sales. And not all markdowns are taken to dispose of slow-selling goods. The skillful buyer uses the markdown to promote merchandise for special sale occasions, as well as for in-store sale events.

A proper understanding of the reasons for a markdown, and the development of skills in the application of the markdown in the merchandising process, can provide the merchant with "a golden key to profit."

[2] Importance
to Overall Operation

The importance of the markdown figure and its effect upon the (1) closing inventory, (2) cumulative mark-on percent, (3) initial mark-on percent, (4) maintained mark-on percent, (5) profit, (6) open-to-buy, (7) shrinkage, (8) gross margin percent, and (9) turnover can best be realized by the illustrative problems and explanations that follow.

It should be realized that markdowns taken during a period apply to both merchandise sold during the period and to merchandise on hand at the close of the period. It is quite possible that all of the marked-down merchandise was sold, or only a part of it was sold, or none of it was sold. It is more likely that some of the marked-down inventory was sold and some of it is still remaining in inventory. The inventory itself is comprised of some merchandise that has not been marked down and some that has been marked down. In essence, then, a part of the inventory will carry a higher mark-on than that portion of the inventory which has been reduced. Nevertheless, the cumulative mark-on percent (the total mark-on derived from both inventories) is applied to the entire inventory.

The expression "cost or market, whichever is lower" indicates that, when the cumulative mark-on percent is applied to that portion of the inventory which has been marked down, the resultant cost is nearer to the current market value of the merchandise rather than to the actual cost of the merchandise. The portion of the inventory that has not been marked down approximates the actual cost.

The retail method of inventory suggests that when an item has been marked down there should be a corresponding markdown of the cost value of the merchandise. In other words, the cost and retail values should be reduced proportionately to reflect the new lower retail price and the new lower market value of the merchandise were it to be repurchased.

The effect of a markdown on the closing inventory can be illustrated with the following example.

Effect of Markdown on the Closing Inventory

Suppose $1,200 worth of merchandise was purchased to retail for a total of $2,000 at a mark-on of 40 percent. One thousand dollars of the merchandise is sold at regular prices. The remaining $1,000 of merchandise was marked down to $800.

Then:

	COST	RETAIL	% MARK-ON
Purchases	$1,200	$ 2,000	40%
Sales		− 1,000	
Closing Retail Inventory		$ 1,000	
Markdowns		− 200	
Closing Inventory After Markdowns and Sales		$ 800 × (100% − 40%)	
Closing Inventory at Cost	$ 480		

Thus, the derived cost is $480, whereas the actual retail value of the closing inventory ($1,000 × 60%) was $600. Therefore, the stock did not depreciate $200 (the retail markdown) but only $120 ($600 − $480 = $120).

Markdowns that are not properly controlled because of careless or improper recording can inflate or deflate the amount of the closing inventory. To illustrate:

Assuming the figures in a department to be:

B.O.M. Inventory	$50,000
Purchases	10,000
Sales	40,000
Markdowns	3,000
Shortages	1,000

If the proper amount of markdowns are recorded, the closing inventory would be:

B.O.M. Inventory	$ 50,000	
Purchases	+ 10,000	
Total Merchandise Handled		$60,000
Sales	$40,000	
Markdowns	+ 3,000	
Shortages	+ 1,000	
		− 44,000
Closing Book Inventory		$ 16,000

If the markdowns are understated by $1,000, then:

B.O.M. Inventory	$ 50,000	
Purchases	+ 10,000	
Total Merchandise Handled		$60,000
Sales	$40,000	
Markdowns	+ 2,000	
Shortages	+ 1,000	
		−$43,000
Closing Book Inventory		$17,000

If the markdowns are overstated by $1,000, then:

B.O.M. Inventory	$ 50,000	
Purchases	+ 10,000	
Total Merchandise Handled		$ 60,000
Sales	$ 40,000	
Markdowns	+ 4,000	
Shortages	+ 1,000	
		− 45,000
Closing Book Inventory		$ 15,000

Therefore, understated markdowns increase the amount of the closing book inventory, while overstated markdowns decrease the amount of the closing book inventory.

Effect of the Markdown on the Cumulative Mark-on Percent

The dollar cumulative mark-on is the difference between the total cost and the total retail value of the merchandise handled during a period, including the inventory on hand at the beginning of the period. The cumulative mark-on percent is this dollar difference as it relates to the total dollar-cumulative amount of merchandise at retail.

The factors that are included in the computation of the cumulative mark-on dollars and the resultant cumulative mark-on percent are indicated in the illustration on page 14. It should be noted from the illustration that markdowns and markdown cancellations have no effect on the cumulative mark-on, dollars or percentage, since they are not included in the determination of the cumulative mark-on. A closer examination of the figures will reveal that the cumulative mark-on includes the preparation of the inventory plus any items that would tend to increase the retail value of the inventory (freight charges, additional markups, purchases). Since markdowns would have the effect of reducing the retail value of the inventory, they are not entered in the computations.

Effect of the Markdown on the Initial Mark-on Percent

The mark-on is the difference between the cost and the retail price:

$$\$ R - \$ C = \$ MO$$

This mark-on must be sufficient to provide for the expected expenses, markdowns, stock shortages, employees' discounts, and alteration expenses if the expected net profit is to be realized.

	COST	RETAIL	CUMULATIVE MARKUP DOLLARS	CUMULATIVE MARKUP %
Opening Inventory	$ 50,000	$ 80,000		
Purchases	+ 40,000	+ 80,000		
Freight Charges To Be Paid by the Store	+ 1,000	—		
Additional Markups	—	+ 3,000		
Transfers-in	+ 10,000	+ 15,000		
Total Additions	$110,000	$178,000		
Returns to Vendors		−$5,000 −$9,000		
Markup Cancellations		— − 1,000		
Transfers-out		−15,000 −25,000		
Net Subtractions	$ 20,000	$35,000		
Total Merchandise Handled	$ 90,000	$143,000	$53,000	37.06%

Cumulative Mark-On Dollars = Total Mdse. Handled at Retail − Total Mdse. Handled at Cost
$$= \$143,000 - \$90,000$$
$$= \$53,000$$

% Cumulative Mark-On $= \dfrac{\text{Cumulative Mark-On Dollars}}{\text{Total Merchandise Handled at Retail}}$

$$= \frac{\$53,000}{\$143,000}$$
$$= 37.06\%$$

The retail price a merchant places on his merchandise is the result both of his past experiences and of his evaluation of future business conditions. It represents the retail price at which he hopes he will be able to sell his merchandise. While the retail price is expressed in dollars and cents on the price ticket, the merchant computes the initial or first mark-on as a percentage of the retail price. Thus, an item that costs the retailer one dollar and that he sells for two dollars represents a mark-on of one dollar ($2 − $1 = $1) or, expressed as a mark-on percent, the one-dollar mark-on is 50 percent of the retail price of two dollars.

As long as the operation stays within the limits of the planned figures, the retailer has a good chance to fulfill his expectations. If he exceeds the planned figures, then his planned profit may not materialize. To illustrate:

A department has the following planned figures:

Planned Sales	$100,000
Operating Expenses	35,000
Alteration Expenses	2,000
Markdowns	8,000
Employees' Discounts	1,000
Stock Shortages	1,000
Cash Discounts	4,000
Net Profit	4,000

Then:

$$\text{Initial Mark-On \%} = \frac{\text{Operating Expenses} + \text{Alteration Expenses} + \text{Net Profit} + \text{Markdowns} + \text{Employees' Discount} + \text{Stock Shortages} + \text{Cash Discounts}}{\text{Sales} + \text{Markdowns} + \text{Employees' Discounts} + \text{Stock Shortages}}$$

$$= \frac{\$35,000 + \$2,000 + \$4,000 + \$8,000 + \$1,000 + \$1,000 - \$4,000}{\$100,000 + \$8,000 + \$1,000 + \$1,000}$$

$$= \frac{\$\ 47,000}{\$110,000}$$

$$= 42.73\%$$

If the retailer realizes a 42.73 percent mark-on, he will be able to meet his expenses and obtain the profit he desires. But the key to this realization is dependent upon the retailer's ability to control his markdowns.

Using the same figures, what effect would an excessive mark-down figure have on the initial mark-on percent?

Assume that the markdowns increased to $9,000 instead of the planned $8,000. Then:

$$= \frac{\$35,000 + \$2,000 + \$4,000 + \$9,000 + \$1,000 + \$1,000 - \$4,000}{\$100,000 + \$9,000 + \$1,000 + \$1,000}$$
$$= \frac{\$ \ 48,000}{\$111,000}$$
$$= 43.24\%$$

As the markdowns increase, the need for a greater initial mark-on percent becomes apparent if the planned profit is to be realized.

Since a higher mark-on may not be possible, the retailer's salvation lies in his ability to reduce the expenses or the stock shortage in order to offset the increase in markdowns.

The Effect of the Markdown on the Maintained Mark-On

The initial mark-on percent has been previously described as the original or "hoped-for" mark-on. The maintained mark-on percent is the actual mark-on obtained after markdowns have been taken. To illustrate:

A buyer purchases 200 dresses at $10 each ($2,000), which he retails at $20 each. Because of competition, he decides to reduce the price of the 200 dresses to $15 each. This represents a markdown of $5 per dress or a total markdown of $1,000 (200 × $5).

Then:

$$\$R = \$C + \$MO$$
$$\$4,000 = \$2,000 + \$2,000$$

for an initial mark-on percent of 50 percent. Because:

$$\% \, MO = \frac{\$MO}{\$R}$$
$$= \frac{\$2,000}{\$4,000}$$
$$= 50\%$$

As a result of the markdown:

$$\$R = \$C + \$MO$$
$$\$3,000 = \$4,000 + \$1,000$$

The mark-on is now $33\frac{1}{3}$ percent, because:

$$\%MO = \frac{\$MO}{\$R}$$
$$= \frac{\$1,000}{\$3,000}$$
$$= 33\frac{1}{3}\%$$

But since the lost mark-on of $1,000 contains the expected profit, the actual loss to the retailer is the cost value of the markdown, or the lost mark-on less the expected profit.

$ Actual Loss = $ Mark-On Lost × % Complement of Initial
$$\text{Mark-On}$$
$$= \$1,000 \times 50\%$$
$$= \$500$$

So, when the 200 dresses are reduced from $20 to $15, $1,000 is lost at retail but only $500 at cost. The difference then between the initial mark-on percent and the maintained mark-on percent is the cost of the markdown.

% Cost of Markdown = % Initial Mark-On − % Maintained
$$\text{Mark-On}$$
$$= 50\% - 33\tfrac{1}{3}\%$$
$$= 16\tfrac{2}{3}\%$$

Proof:

$$\% \text{ MD} = \frac{\$MD}{\$ \text{ Net Sales}}$$
$$= \frac{\$1,000}{\$3,000}$$
$$= 33\tfrac{1}{3}\%$$

With this understanding, the buyer can compute the maximum dollar markdown available to him for a period. To illustrate:

The planned figures for a department are:

Initial Mark-On	40%
Maintained Mark-On	34%

Since:

% Cost of Markdowns = % Initial Mark-On − % Maintained
$$\text{Mark-On}$$
$$= 40\% - 34\%$$
$$= 6\%$$

Then, the retail value of the markdown can be determined:

$$\% \text{ Retail of Markdowns} = \frac{\% \text{ Cost of Markdown}}{\% \text{ Complement of Initial Mark-On}}$$

$$= \frac{6\%}{60\%}$$

$$= 10\%$$

If the planned sales for the period were $100,000, then:

$$\$ \text{ Markdown} = \$ \text{ Planned Sales} \times \% \text{ Retail Markdown}$$

$$= \$100,000 \times 10\%$$

$$= \$10,000$$

Similarly, a buyer can determine his resultant maintained mark-on if the percent of initial mark-on and the percent markdowns (at retail) are known. To illustrate, assume:

$$\% \text{ Initial Mark-On} \quad = 40\%$$
$$\% \text{ Markdowns (at Retail)} = 10\%$$

Then:

$$\% \text{ Cost of Markdowns} = \% \text{ Markdowns} \times \% \text{ Complement of Initial Mark-On}$$

$$= 10\% \times 60\%$$

$$= 6\%$$

Then:

$$\% \text{ Maintained Mark-On} = \% \text{ Initial Mark-On} - \% \text{ Cost of Markdown}$$

$$= 40\% - 6\%$$

$$= 34\%$$

A reduction in the retail price with the same purchase or cost price can have the effect of reducing the mark-on.

For example:

A man's jacket, now in stock, retails for $50 for a mark-on of 40 percent. The jacket is repurchased at $30 to retail for $40. What is the new mark-on percent?

$$\begin{aligned} \$ \text{ Cost of Jacket Retailing at } \$50 &= \$ \text{ Retail} \times \% \text{ Complement} \\ &\qquad \text{of Mark-On} \\ &= \$50 \times 60\% \\ &= \$30 \end{aligned}$$

If the cost remains at $30 and the jacket is retailed at $40, then:

$$\begin{aligned} \% \text{ Mark-On} &= \frac{\$ \text{ Mark-On}}{\$ \text{ Retail}} \\ &= \frac{\$10}{\$40} \\ &= 25\% \end{aligned}$$

The reduction in the retail price of $10 has resulted in a loss of 15 percent in the original mark-on.

The resultant mark-on from these two transactions would be as follows:

$$\begin{aligned} \text{Total } \$ \text{ Cost} &= 2 \text{ Jackets at } \$30 \text{ Each} \\ &= \$60 \\ \text{Total } \$ \text{ Retail} &= 1 \text{ Jacket at } \$50 \\ &\qquad 1 \text{ Jacket at } \$40 \\ &= \$90 \\ \text{Net } \% \text{ Mark-On} &= \frac{\$ \text{ Mark-On}}{\$ \text{ Retail}} \\ &= \frac{\$30}{\$90} \\ &= 33\tfrac{1}{3}\% \end{aligned}$$

Effect of Markdown on Profit

While markdowns have no effect upon the cumulative mark-on percent, they do affect the profit obtained when they are controlled. To illustrate:

If the cumulative mark-on of a department is 40 percent and the markdowns are reduced by $1,000, the additional profit would be the actual cost of the markdowns eliminated. Thus:

$ Cost of Markdowns = $ Markdowns Reduced × % Complement Initial Cumulative Mark-On
= $1,000 × 60%
= $600

The additional profit gained is, therefore, $600.

Effect of Markdowns on the Open-To-Buy

The basic method of arriving at the open-to-buy is the difference between the dollar inventory needed and the dollar inventory available:

Available	Needed
Stock on Hand	Planned Sales
Merchandise on Order	Markdown
	Stock Shortages
	E.O.M. Stock

Any increase in a figure in the "Need" column will reduce the retail value of the inventory. Therefore, by taking more markdowns, more open-to-buy is made available. To illustrate:

Available		*Needed*	
Stock on Hand	$70,000	Planned Sales	$50,000
Merchandise on		Planned Markdowns	5,000
Order	10,000		
		Planned Stock	
		Shortages	500
Total Merchandise			
Available	$80,000	Planned E.O.M.	
		Stock	25,000
		Total Merchandise	
		Needed	$80,500

The difference between the need of $80,500 and what is available ($80,000) indicates an open-to-buy of only $500.

Additional markdowns taken during the period will have the effect of increasing the open-to-buy. Using the same figures, but increasing the markdowns by $2,000, we see:

Available		*Needed*	
Stock on Hand	$70,000	Planned Sales	$50,000
Merchandise on		Planned Markdowns	7,000
Order	10,000		
		Planned Stock	
		Shortages	500
Total Merchandise			
Available	$80,000	Planned E.O.M.	
		Stock	25,000
		Total Merchandise	
		Needed	$82,500

The difference between the need of $82,500 and what is

available ($80,000) now indicates an open-to-buy of $2,500.

Since markdowns are planned and controlled, this technique is not likely to be recommended for obtaining additional open-to-buy money.

Effect of Markdown on Shrinkage or Shortage

If a buyer fails to record a markdown, it will result in an inflated closing or book inventory. This action in turn creates a shortage. To illustrate:

Opening Inventory at Retail	$20,000
Purchases at Retail	40,000
Net Sales	35,000
Net Markdowns	2,000

A physical inventory was taken and revealed an inventory of $20,000. Then:

Opening Inventory at Retail	$ 20,000	
Purchases at Retail	+40,000	
Total Merchandise Handled		$60,000
Net Sales	$ 35,000	
Net Markdowns	+ 2,000	
		− 37,000
Closing Book Inventory		$ 23,000

Since:

The physical inventory is	− 20,000	
The shortage is		$ 3,000

Let us examine the effect on these figures if the buyer recorded only $1,500 of markdowns and failed to record

$500 of markdowns. Then:

Opening Inventory at Retail	$ 20,000	
Purchases at Retail	+ 40,000	
Total Merchandise Handled		$60,000
Net Sales	$ 35,000	
Net Markdowns	+ 1,500	
		− $36,500
Closing Book Inventory		$23,500

Since:

The physical inventory is	− $20,000	
The shortage is		$ 3,500

Therefore, an understated markdown figure or a failure to record all markdowns will increase the shortage and overstate the closing book inventory. Conversely, an over-stated markdown figure will decrease the shortage and understate the closing book inventory. To illustrate:

Assume that the original net markdowns of $2,000 was overstated to $2,500. Then:

Opening Inventory at Retail	$ 20,000	
Purchases at Retail	+ 40,000	
Total Merchandise Handled		$60,000
Net Sales	$ 35,000	
Net Markdowns	+ 2,500	
		− $37,500
Closing Book Inventory		$22,500

Since:

The physical inventory is	− $20,000	
The shortage is		$ 2,500

Therefore, the closing inventory is understated by $500 and the shortage is understated by $500.

Effect of Markdowns on Gross Margin

The gross margin is the difference between the net sales and the total merchandise costs. It is expressed as a percentage of net sales. We have seen that the cost of the reductions (markdowns, discounts to employees, shortages), when subtracted from the initial mark-on, produces the maintained mark-on. The gross margin is determined when the alteration costs are subtracted and the cash discounts are added. To illustrate:

A department shows the following figures:

Initial Mark-On	40%
Markdowns	8%
Alteration Costs	2%
Cash Discounts Earned	4%

Then:

% Maintained Mark-On = % Initial Mark-On − % Cost of Markdown

$$= 40\% - (8\% \times 60\%)$$
$$= 40\% - 4.80\%$$
$$= 35.20\%$$

And:

$$\% \text{ Gross Margin} = \% \text{ Maintained Mark-On} - \text{Alteratin Cost}$$
$$+ \% \text{ Cash Discounts Earned}$$
$$= 35.20\% - 2\% + 4\%$$
$$= 33.20\% + 4\%$$
$$= 37.20\%$$

An increase in the markdown percent will have the effect of reducing the gross margin percent. To illustrate:

Using the same figures, let us assume an increase in the markdowns to 9 percent. Then:

$$\% \text{ Maintained Mark-On} = \% \text{ Initial Mark-On} - \% \text{ Cost of}$$
$$\text{Markdown}$$
$$= 40\% - (9\% \times 60\%)$$
$$= 40\% - 5.40\%$$
$$= 34.60\%$$

And:

$$\% \text{ Gross Margin} = \% \text{ Maintained Mark-On} - \% \text{Alteration}$$
$$\text{Costs} + \% \text{Cash Discounts Earned}$$
$$= 34.60\% - 2\% + 4\%$$
$$= 32.60\% + 4\%$$
$$= 36.60\%$$

Therefore, an increase of 1 percent in markdowns is the equivalent of a reduction in the gross margins of .60 percent (which is the cost of the 1 percent increase in markdowns). A decrease in the markdown percent will have the effect of increasing the gross margin. To illustrate:

Using the same figures, let us assume a decrease in the markdowns to 7 percent. Then:

$$\% \text{ Maintained Mark-On} = \% \text{ Initial Mark-On} - \% \text{ Cost of}$$
$$\text{Markdowns}$$
$$= 40\% - (7\% \times 60\%)$$
$$= 40\% - 4.20\%$$
$$= 35.80\%$$

And:

$$\% \text{ Gross Margin} = \% \text{ Maintained Mark-On} - \% \text{ Alteration}$$
$$\text{Costs} + \% \text{ Cash Discounts Earned}$$
$$= 35.80\% - 2\% + 4\%$$
$$= 33.80\% + 4\%$$
$$= 37.80\%$$

Therefore, a decrease of 1 percent in markdowns is the equivalent of an increase in the gross margin of .60 percent (which is the cost of the 1 percent decrease in markdowns).

Effect of Markdowns on Turnover

There is a direct relationship between good turnover and a low markdown percentage: the faster the stock turnover, the smaller the percentage of markdowns. A slow turnover frequently is responsible for a higher markdown percentage. However, overemphasis on the stock turnover can increase the markdown percent. The stock turnover is determined by:

$$\text{Stock Turnover} = \frac{\text{Net Sales}}{\text{Average Inventory at Retail}}$$

To realize the planned stock turnover, the retailer can make use of several approaches:

1. Achieve the net sales and average inventory figures as planned.

2. Obtain an increase in the net sales with no increase in the average inventory.

3. Obtain a decrease in the average inventory with no increase in the net sales.

4. Obtain a decrease in the net sales and decrease in the average inventory.

To illustrate:

Assume the following planned figures for a department:

Sales $100,000
Average Retail Inventory $ 25,000

Then:

$$\text{Stock Turnover} = \frac{\$100,000}{\$\ 25,000}$$
$$= 4$$

Approach 1. If the planned figures are realized, then the planned stock turnover of 4 will be realized, as illustrated.

Approach 2. If the sales are increased by 10 percent, with no increase or decrease in the average inventory, then:

$$\text{Stock Turnover} = \frac{\$110,000}{\$\ 25,000}$$
$$= 4.4$$

an increase of .4 in the turnover.

Approach 3. If the average inventory is decreased by 10 percent with no increase or decrease in sales, then:

$$\text{Stock Turnover} = \frac{\$100,000}{\$\ 22,500}$$
$$= 4.4$$

an increase of .4 in the turnover.

Approach 4. If the sales decrease 10 percent and the average inventory decreases 10 percent, then:

$$\text{Stock Turnover} = \frac{\$90,000}{\$22,500}$$

resulting in the planned turnover of 4.

However, if the sales decrease by 10 percent while the average inventory increases by 10 percent, then:

$$\text{Stock Turnover} = \frac{\$90,000}{\$27,500}$$
$$= 3.27$$

In order to accelerate the sales and to move the excess inventory for the purpose of achieving the desired turnover of 4, it will be necessary to mark down the inventory. If the inventory is reduced by 5 percent and it results in an increase of sales of 5 percent, then:

$$\text{Stock Turnover} = \frac{\$94,500}{\$26,125}$$
$$= 3.62$$

While there is an improvement in the turnover of .35, it is obvious that additional markdowns would be required to raise the turnover to 4. Thus, if the additional markdowns amounted to 5 percent and assuming another 5 percent increase in sales, then:

$$\text{Stock Turnover} = \frac{\$99,225.00}{\$25,818.75}$$
$$= 3.84$$

To achieve the desired turnover of 4, additional markdowns would be required. Therefore, since a slow turnover frequently is responsible for a higher markdown percent and consequently a smaller return on the investment, the keys to a good turnover with a low markdown percent are:

1. To stock wanted items, which will result in a faster turnover, which in turn means fresher merchandise. Volume is increased because stocks are fresh, new, and interesting.

2. To be overstocked means higher markdowns, as much as 20 percent over the "normal." The average inventory can be decreased while realizing an increase in sales through quicker and better deliveries of needed items, thereby eliminating overstocking.

3. Inventorying a department through a basic stock system can eliminate the need to buy too far ahead, thereby increasing the possibility of a higher turnover with a lower markdown percent.

4. Greater concentration on basic items and best sellers and less concentration on "fringe items" and variety can lessen the need for markdowns while improving the turnover with a lower inventory.

5. With fashion merchandise, the shorter the period during which merchandise is in stock, the less the risk that the item will deteriorate or go out of fashion. Selling enthusiasm is generally lost when merchandise moves slowly. The poor turnover will result in increased markdowns and profit losses.

In the final analysis, turnover is the consequence of a good merchandising job based on the normally accepted practices of good merchandise planning and control. If improvement in the performance of those functions that improve turnover can be achieved, then lower markdowns with increased profits will be the reward.

[3] Classification of Markdowns

A study of the price-change forms used by the various retail operations indicates that markdowns can generally be classified as follows:

1. In order to dispose of the remainders of merchandise purchased by the store for special sale purposes, the markdowns that are taken are identified as *promotional purchase remainders*. These items may be advertised as irregulars, job lots, and closeouts.

2. Markdowns taken on regular stock because the rate of sale is slower than experience indicates that type of merchandise should sell are identified as *slow-moving* or *inactive stock markdowns*.

3. At times retailers mark down regular stock merchandise for special sales. At the conclusion of the sale the merchandise is returned to its regular price. Such markdowns are identified as *special sales from stock markdowns*.

4. Markdowns taken to meet competitive situations; markdowns taken to adjust the current retail prices to changing wholesale prices; and markdowns taken when price lines are adjusted downward are classified as *price-adjustment markdowns*.

5. The classification of markdowns listed as *broken assortments* and *remnants markdowns* includes those odd pieces of merchandise remaining from the sale of regular

stock that is no longer to be stocked by the store. These items are generally labeled as odds and ends.

6. Since most merchandise items are handled by customers and salespeople many times in the daily selling process, it is possible that some of these items may become soiled, damaged, or shopworn. This is especially true of those stores in which most of the merchandise is exposed, very little of it under glass. Those stores that are dedicated to service are likely to have fewer items to list under these headings. The markdowns taken for these reasons are identified as *shopworn, soiled,* or *damaged markdowns.*

7. At times an interested customer may, if the retail price is reduced, wish to purchase a stock item that is damaged. At other times a customer may complain about his purchase for one reason or another. Adjustment of the complaint may be made by returning a portion of the price paid by the customer at the time of the purchase. Both these adjustments are classified as *allowance-to-customer markdowns.*

8. If the department is aware that an item has been stolen, or is assumed to be stolen by virtue of its absence from stock with no record of a sale, the store will require that a markdown be taken to remove the item from stock. The markdown is classified as a *stolen markdown.*

9. "Breakage" or "salvage" refers to those items of stock merchandise which have been so damaged as to render them completely unsalable or unrepairable. Customarily these items are listed on a separate, authorization-for-salvage markdown sheet, although many stores record this item on their regular price-change form. The markdown is classified as a *salvage markdown.*

There are some transactions that reduce the retail value

of the inventory but are not generally classified as a markdown:

1. Discounts to such special groups as teachers and
other groups.
2. Policy adjustments, which consist of allowances to
customers to maintain their goodwill, and which are classified as an operating expense.
3. Allowances from vendors when the retail prices are
reduced as a consequence of the change in the wholesale
price. Such reductions are generally adjustments in the
retail value of the purchases.

Some stores classify their markdowns in a more simplified
manner, as:

1. *Promotional.* These are markdowns taken for advertised or unadvertised in-store events.
2. *Liquidation.* These are markdowns taken to move
slow-selling goods.
3. *Soiled or damaged.* These markdowns are taken for
the same reasons previously stated.
4. *Competition.* These markdowns are taken for the
same reasons previously stated.

The manner in which markdowns are refined for control
purposes will depend upon the nature of the operation
and the purposes for which the information is intended.

[4] Reasons for Markdowns

Some markdowns are necessary, other markdowns are inevitable, but too many markdowns are unnecessary and avoidable; regrettably, the number of reasons causing unnecessary markdowns are greater than all other reasons for markdowns combined. There should be concern and effort on the part of the merchandising personnel involved toward understanding the reasons causing avoidable markdowns, with a view to correcting and improving their professional performance.

Cicero said, "Any man may make a mistake, but none but a fool will continue in it." The key to cutting down unnecessary markdowns lies in the ability of the merchandising management to communicate the necessary attitudes, understanding, knowledge, and skills regarding markdowns to those who are in a position to cause them. The mere signing of a price-change request without patient explanation, discussion, and illustration, in an atmosphere of sincere helpfulness, only tends to perpetuate Cicero's philosophical statement. Merchandise managers have long realized that, next to the important items of rent and payroll, the markdown is the one most serious item in determining whether an operation is to yield a reasonable contribution or not.

It would be a mistake to take refuge and satisfaction in a markdown result that would reflect an improvement over the previous year's markdown performance. Buyer training in this area must be on a continuous basis if the weaknesses in the buyer's attitudes, understanding, and knowledge are to be corrected, improved, and professionalized. Complacency as the result of an improvement in markdown performance, no matter how slight, could make it difficult, if not impossible, to restructure the avoidable buying procedures and practices that create unnecessary markdowns.

Not all of the avoidable markdowns are caused by the ineptness of buyers. Merchandise managers contribute their share to the creation of the markdown and to the perpetuation of weaknesses.

An examination of the reasons for markdowns will serve to focus attention on the actions that contribute to the need for a markdown.

Reasons for Markdowns Created by the Merchandise Manager

1. Pressuring the buyer to get the cooperative advertising money, without regard to the merits of the purchase. On paper, the net advertising result makes pleasant reading, but the prior stock report will not. The markdown has been created, and now the attitude of the buyer is one of retribution, rather than contribution. The purchase was made to satisfy the demands of the merchandise manager, not the needs of the consumer—solving the merchandise manager's problem, but forming one for the

buyer. Because he has purchased "dead stock," destined for the markdown table, a bite has been taken out of his open-to-buy that may prevent him from purchasing needed items.

2. Confirming reorders without requesting a distribution stock count of the merchandise on hand by color, size, and quantity, in addition to the rate of sale and history of the item. Too often, vendor representatives supposedly take stock counts, and in many instances make out the reorder for merchandise. Surrendering this buyer responsibility makes possible unnecessary reorders, and the reorder of quantities not legitimately based on need. A closer scrutiny of the stock and sales history will compel the buyer to review his own situation and make for more intelligent use of the open-to-buy.

3. Confirming new orders that do not indicate a description of the item, a reason for the purchase, the type of merchandise, the retail price, and the expected mark-on. The procedure of confirming new orders affords the merchandise manager an opportunity to determine the need for the item, the timing of the purchase, the reasonableness of the quantity, the selection of delivery date and cancellation date, and the correctness of the retail price—and, in addition, prevent attempts by the buyer to open new, untried but questionable resources. While marginal producers are more apt to be ready for a "deal," the chances for overpricing and unwillingness to accept returns for repairs, credit, or exchange (after the invoice has been paid) are more likely. The merchandise manager who scrutinizes new orders is in a position to prevent future markdowns through the intelligent use of his power of confirmation.

4. Failure to insist on periodic prior stock reports, failure to review these reports with the buyer immediately, failure to follow up prior price-change reports mutually agreed upon, and failure to visit the selling floor (where possible) to appraise the action taken to sell the merchandise. Merchants agree that markdowns taken during the season provide the merchandise with a better acceptance possibility than merchandise that is carried over to the next season. Prior or aged items, religiously inventoried according to a predetermined schedule, discussed, and concerning which an agreed-upon plan of action is forcefully supported, can very effectively contribute to a reduction in the extent of markdowns. Delays in inventorying these items, and delays in discussion between the merchandise manager and the buyer, only tend to increase the amount of markdowns that will finally be needed to move the stock. Merchandise managers who establish target "must" dates for the prior inventory usually find that the buyer is moved to markdown action before the inventory is submitted. The reasons for the buyer's desire to submit an inventory that has indications of buyer-action already taken are obvious. Vacillation or indifference on the part of the merchandise manager to the inventory schedule can be very costly.

5. Failure to review the open-order file in order to evaluate, with the buyer, the need for past-due merchandise and the poor delivery of needed items. Merchandise managers will agree that canceling an order merely because it is past delivery time should not be done mechanically. Despite the fact that the merchandise will be late in arriving, it may still sell out. Therefore each cancellation should be considered on its merits. Merchandise managers

will also agree that the store that receives the item first has the best chance to be the first to reorder, so buyers who discipline vendors with a view toward early delivery avoid the risk of receiving merchandise when it is ready for a markdown.

A review of the open orders gives the merchandise manager a reason for stiffening buyers' lax attitudes, with regard both to proper delivery and to the cancellation of items that have passed the peak of selling opportunities. The establishment of a weekly order-review schedule, strictly adhered to, will force the buyer to correct conditions before his scheduled meeting with the merchandise manager. Thus, unnecessary markdowns are reduced and avoided.

6. Failure to review the number of returns to vendor, for credit or repair during a particular period, as well as the number of repairs out-of-stock for an extended period of time. Probably one of the great weaknesses of the merchandising operation is the inattention given to the length of time stock merchandise is allowed to remain at the cleaner's or vendor's. By the time these items are returned to the store—and in many instances their number is considerable—it is past selling time—time for a markdown. Obviously, vendors will be able to supply the buyer with a sufficient number of excuses for the two- or three-month delay, but merchandise managers who review these open items on a regular schedule find that the buyer can obtain better and faster results if the vendor applies as much attention to repairs as he does to new orders.

Merchandise managers who insist upon a daily written report from the vendor return room of the packages that have been sent to vendors but that have been returned from vendors to the store for such reasons as "Refused to Accept," "Send to Factory," "Wrong Address," etc., will find another effective weapon to combat unnecessary or avoidable markdowns.

7. Failure to review with the buyer the condition of the stockrooms and the stock drawers. A disorganized stockroom, which makes it difficult for salespeople to find an item, will not only discourage selling but will reduce the productivity of salespeople. The item will probably turn up as a markdown when someone decides to organize the room—and what salesperson hasn't exclaimed at least once, "Where have these been? I could have sold a million last week!" One of the shocking reasons for markdowns is merchandise that is "buried" in stock drawers and that never sees the light of day. A workable procedure to show every new item to every salesperson (including part-timers) will go a long way to curing this ill.

Again, planned scheduled inspections, with the buyer notified in advance of the date, will provide the stimulus necessary to get the stockroom into shape and stock drawers inspected. There are markdowns in the stockroom and markdowns in the stock drawers, and unless some procedure is developed to eliminate these "hidden" markdowns, they are certain to contribute considerably to the avoidable-markdown problem.

8. Failure to determine why the buyer has not taken any markdowns or very little markdowns during a period. Merchandise managers who maintain a check list of the buyer's activities can prevent markdowns by requesting a markdown sheet from the buyer. This will compel the buyer to examine his stock for needed markdowns and prevent him from "saving" his markdowns for the end of

the month. It should be realized that the buyer's rationale
for taking markdowns may not be consistent with sound
merchandising practices. Only an alert merchandise manager, through a check list, can correct false understandings,
thereby removing a cause for unnecessary markdowns.

Since markdowns are usually planned, there is no valid
reason for the delay in taking one. There is a need for a
sense of urgency in taking markdowns when they should
be taken. Excessive markdowns can be avoided through
a procedure of "reminders" by the merchandise manager.

9. Failure to evaluate, with the buyer, a markdown
request (price-change form) to determine the need for
the markdown, the timing of the markdown, and the
amount of the markdown. How many price-change sheets
are countersigned by the merchandise managers without
examination of the request? How much in markdown
dollars could be saved if closer scrutiny, followed by discussion, was given to price-change requests? One merchandise manager insists that his buyers discuss their plan
for markdowns with him before the request is submitted.
Such discussion may provide suggestions for clearing the
goods without a markdown, or for determining the extent
of the markdown.

Some buyers are addicted to markdowns as a relief from
their merchandise problems. Most creative minds can
discover less costly relief, and discussion can provide
the basis for this creativity. To sign a markdown request
without professional perusal is to be a "rubber-stamp"
merchandise manager. It is also unfair to the buyer, since
it deprives him of the merchandise manager's superior
skill and expertise.

10. Failure to review buyer's visits to competitors and

to review comparison shopping reports. Pride does not allow some buyers to take any notice of their competitors. They are jealous and prejudiced against their rivals, and would prefer to underestimate them. But wise merchants know that buyers must, at every moment, know what his competitors are doing, what merchandise they are showing, what the retail prices are, how the merchandise is being highlighted, and how they are going after business. A true estimate of competitors' strengths and weaknesses will make it possible to beat them at their own game.

Seasoned merchandisers will testify that not only should a buyer know what his competitors are doing all the time, but should never underestimate anything a competitor does. However, since buyers are generally prejudiced against their competitors, investigations must be made by an objective agency. For this reason stores maintain, at great expense, comparison shopping departments, whose function it is to know at all times what other stores are featuring and selling, and how the quality and prices compare with their own stock of goods. A store that consumers find wanting in meeting the designs of the competition, will pay for their pride and jealousy in excessive and unnecessary markdowns.

11. Making merchandise commitments at home or abroad without prior discussion with the buyer. Someone once said, "A good executive is one who gets his nose into everything, but his fingers into nothing." Invading a buyer's open-to-buy, and at the same time denying him the right of dissent, is for a merchandise man to get his fingers into everything, contrary to the stated axiom. Even if the buyer thought the merchandise purchased was a worthwhile item, his personal resentment at the invasion of his

domain would destine the item for the markdown rack. Some executives are overcome when they visit exotic lands, but they learn after a while that the item might not have the same mystique or appeal to the stores' customers. Executives would serve the cause of unnecessary markdowns best by enjoying their vacation in foreign lands and forgetting about the "store."

12. Pressuring the buyer into quantities of merchandise for a planned event with high mark-on requirements. If merchandise for a sales event is not taken from regular stock, then it must be specially purchased. The item to be offered must be a "value," since the purpose of a sale is to give the customer an item priced lower than regularly. If the buyer has to give a "value" and at the same time obtain regular mark-ons, then he must usually buy goods below his regular standards of quality, workmanship, and material. While the merchandise offering is below regular price levels, experience indicates that on sale days customers only buy approximately 60 percent to 70 percent of the sale items and 30 percent to 40 percent of regular-priced goods. This means that considerable sale goods will remain that the buyer cannot mesh into regular price levels because the merchandise would suffer by comparison. And, since the buyer does not plan to reorder the item, the result is a markdown.

13. Failure to review buying plans with the buyer to insure intelligent planning, timing, delivery, and presentation. If we accept the role of the merchandise manager as that of a merchandise "guidance counselor" to the buyer, then the possibilities of unnecessary markdowns can be minimized. Mutual discussions ahead of the buying period, supported by the expertise of the merchandise

manager, can provide the buyer with a schedule or time-table that will develop his merchandising skills and reduce the chances of his creating markdowns. This guidance can commence with teaching the buyer the need for keeping proper records of past experiences, then, step by step, proceed through the final clearance of the merchandise. For merchandise seen in time, purchased in time, and presented in time will result in the greatest possible sales with the least amount of markdowns.

It has been said that "a buyer without a plan is no buyer at all." But it would be incorrect to assume that all buyers are capable of planning. The merchandise guidance counselor can provide this "know-how" and avoid unnecessary markdowns.

Naturally, not all of the reasons listed here are applicable to all types of retail operations. Decentralization of merchandising responsibilities and a degree of self-autonomy are important factors. But regardless of the situation, procedures should be established that will accomplish the aims of sound markdown practices and correct the bad ones, as expressed here.

Reasons for Markdowns Created by the Buyer

1. Buying from imagination rather than from facts. Buyers who go into the market without records, or with faulty records, cannot buy intelligently. There is no substitute for factual information from which to make im-

portant buying decisions. The buyer has a moral and ethical obligation, both to his customers and to his store, to visit the market armed and fortified with all of the necessary information needed to buy the best merchandise at the lowest possible prices, merchandise that will provide the greatest satisfaction to the customers and the greatest profit to the store. These aims cannot be achieved if the buyer has to draw from memory information about the myriads of styles, colors, sizes, fabrics, quantities, and prices in his stock.

It has been said that "the memory of man is very short." Unnecessary markdowns can be avoided if the buyer does not trust his short memory to spend large sums of money for which he has agreed to be the caretaker.

2. Buying subjectively rather than objectively. As a fundamental axiom of retailing states, "Find out what your customers want, and be sure to have it for them when they want it. Find out what they don't want and be sure not to stock it." The key words here are "what your customers want." If the buyer learns to relate to the wants and needs of those who are going to pay him for the merchandise, namely his customers, then the buyer will be customer-oriented and not self-oriented. Without customers a store has no business. Without business a store has no profit. Without a profit a store cannot function.

The question the buyer must continually ask himself is, "Will it serve the needs of my customer?" If merchandise is stocked based on this criterion, then the possibilities for quick sales and minimal markdowns will be far greater than otherwise. Merchandising history has proven that you cannot force a consumer to buy that which he or she does not want. Therefore, a buyer's personal likes and dislikes must be completely disregarded in the selection of goods if unnecessary markdowns are to be avoided.

3. Failure to relate new items to current inventory. Buyers who fail to realize or anticipate the effect of the introduction of new goods upon items already in stock create unnecessary markdowns. If the new item is going to make the current item in stock less desirable, a severe markdown may result unless a transitional period is considered for disposing of the current stock. The buyer can avoid this markdown by planning the disposition of the current stock before advertising the new item.

4. Indulging in sloppy stockkeeping practices. Avoidable markdowns can be minimized through an intelligent program of stockkeeping, involving the protection of merchandise during the selling day and at night. By working with the vendors on improved methods of packaging; by day-to-day training of department personnel in the handling, stocking, care, and selling of the items; and by setting standards to reduce soilage, breakage, and damage to merchandise, the buyer can avoid markdowns. And he should not overlook the need for developing good practices of stockkeeping and care of stock at the branches. In a store where the merchandise is almost 100 percent exposed, and customers are permitted to search for the merchandise in the stock drawers, the need for corrective measures to reduce the resultant unnecessary markdowns is paramount.

5. Showing poor buying judgment. A buyer is entitled to make some errors in judgment based on incorrect evaluation and appraisal of his customers' buying habits. He is not, however, entitled to make errors in buying judgment by relinquishing the buying decision to the vendor. When

the buyer permits the vendor to make the merchandise selection for him, he is guilty of poor buying judgment. Such vendor expressions as, "I know what you need. Leave it to me," or, "Don't worry, I'll take care of everything," are invitations to profit catastrophe. It makes little difference that the buyer is buying a job lot of merchandise or new items—the principle is the same. A fundamental of merchandising states, "Buyers don't buy, they select." This involves careful examination of each item to insure proper consumer acceptance. To revise slightly a current advertising slogan, "Leave the selection to us," when spoken by a vendor, would guarantee unnecessary markdowns.

Similarly, a buyer who signs an order prepared by a unit control clerk without questioning quantities, colors, sizes, or timing of the order is equally guilty of poor buying judgment.

6. Buying for discount or low price. Once the need for an item has been established, then the factors of delivery time, reorder time, and rate of sale should be the criteria for the quantity to be ordered. Buying in larger quantities than the rate of sale warrants, merely because of the temptations of a discount or a lower price for quantity purchases, can cause serious losses. The possibility of damage, shoplifting, breakage, or soilage can erase all of the gains from the lower price or increased discount. In addition, the added capital investment in the inventory precludes the use of that amount for other merchandise needs or new merchandise items.

To overcome the temptation of buying too large a quantity of goods, merchandise men follow the simple rule of "Buy a little at a time, but buy often." They have found it to be a good prescription for helping buyers who "think big, but can't buy small" to avoid unnecessary markdowns.

7. Permitting odd sizes, colors, and patterns to accumulate. A stock of merchandise is expected to have some odds and ends as a result of the accumulation of odd sizes, colors, patterns, or styles, but some buyers hold on to these items at full price in the hope that some customer will buy the odd item. However, only markdowns can move these items out of stock quickly.

Often the longer these items remain in stock, the more difficult it becomes to find a customer who can use or has a need for the particular item. While it is hoped that the number of such items will be few, failure to recognize them and to act quickly can result in unnecessary markdowns.

8. Attempting to price the merchandise too high. Some merchandise items present opportunities to obtain a higher-than-normal mark-on. However, there is always the possibility of "pricing one's self out of the market," by underestimating the consumer's ability to judge quality and value and at the same time overestimating his willingness to pay the price placed on the item. The resultant markdown may destroy the desirability of the item, while a reasonable price with a reasonable mark-on could have insured its success. Merchandise managers who recognize this possibility are quick to restrain the buyer's eagerness "to make a killing."

9. Buying from too many resources. For a long time, manufacturers and retailers have recognized the advantages of concentrating purchases with a minimum of resources. One large retail operation recently announced that 64 percent of its purchases were made from 10 percent

of its suppliers. Buying from many resources deprives the merchandising mix of continuity. Instead, the department becomes a sales testing laboratory, and the result is "a whole lot of nothing."

Skillful buyers who have learned the importance of concentrating their purchases with fewer resources have also learned that they can reduce unnecessary markdowns.

10. Failure to understand the principles and importance of the three merchandising controls—a basic stock, a model stock, and a well-rounded assortment. The purpose of merchandise management is to maximize sales, minimize stocks, provide more of items that are currently wanted, and to eliminate undesirable merchandise. Therefore, the actions of proper merchandise management will increase the average salescheck and ultimately provide more profit. A buyer who understands the full meaning and value of these significant merchandising controls, and labors to make them effective tools for customer satisfaction, will have taken a giant step toward the reduction of unnecessary markdowns.

Those time-accepted fundamentals, "You can't do business from an empty wagon" and "You can't run a business from the seat of your pants," are at the very heart of the three merchandising tools, and close attention to them will insure a balanced stock based on need, giving the customer what he wants when he wants it.

To be sure, there are hundreds of other reasons leading to markdowns. The ones presented here are considered to be the most significant, the ones requiring the greatest concentration and attention.

[5] Markdown Policies

Business policies are top management's long-range guiding principles to give direction and stability to the organization. Policies are the answers to problems that arise in the course of the operation of the business.

To be effective, and to avoid misunderstanding or ignorance of their existence, the policies are put in writing and made available to everyone concerned with their execution.

Markdown policies relate to the activity of merchandising and are therefore formulated by the merchandising division. An examination of some of these policies will indicate their importance in the overall operation.

While retailers recognize that they "cannot be all things to all people," they must nevertheless be aware of the pricing activities of the competition. Many retailers maintain the policy "that they will not be undersold." The basic factor involved in the formulation of this policy is that the customer's goodwill must be maintained if the store is to retain its competitive position in the community. The approach taken by retailers vary in the implementation of this policy. Some retailers tell the customer that they will have the item shopped, and, if the information supplied by the customer is correct, they will meet the competitive price. It is interesting to note that the customer, in most cases, does not make the purchase at the lower-price store.

Apparently, he would prefer to make the purchase in his "favorite" store.

Other retailers tell the customer to make the purchase at the higher price, after which it will be shopped for comparison and, if correct, the difference will be refunded or credited—the wisdom of which has often been challenged by customers. The markdown policy in this instance concerns itself with three questions: (1) Should the store take the markdown on the one item when a customer complains? or (2) should the entire stock of the item be reduced, even though only one customer has complained? or (3) should the item be removed from sale until the competitor has restored the price?

The first question implies that a markdown will be taken only when a customer complains, otherwise the price will remain higher than that of the competitor. The policy presupposes that all customers will not complain. Those customers who do not complain may assume that the store's prices are generally higher and may so inform their neighbors and friends. However, there may be justifiable reasons why the store will not reduce the retail price of the entire stock of the item. For example, the lower price may be at a store that offers none of the shopping or service advantages rendered by the first store. While the store does not wish to disregard competition on identical items, it recognizes that price alone is not the only factor that moves people to buy. The markdown policy of other stores might include the considerations of beating the competitor's price or taking the item off sale until the storm blows over. In any event, the markdown policy of the store with regard to the competition will determine the extent of the markdown as it affects a buyer's operation. And as far as the matter of customers' unfair requests for credit, refund, or exchange goes, the fundamental principle of building a business, "Lose the argument but win the customer," is practiced by virtually all retailers, although some retailers are more liberal than others when such requests are made by customers.

Those buyers who enjoy a good relationship with their suppliers may be able to avoid the markdown for the return. While some buyers will naturally balk at a liberal customer policy because of the markdown, the management recognizes that this markdown policy can only build a business. When the store accepts the return or makes an allowance to retain the goodwill of the customer, a policy adjustment (which is classified as an operating expense and not as a markdown) is taken.

If the retailer uses the markdown as a "leader" item, the higher-than-normal markdown will probably be included in the planning of the initial mark-on. This same consideration would hold true when the plan is drawn for fashion goods. The markdown would have to be sufficient to compensate for the higher markdowns fashion goods require in order to dispose of the slow sellers.

It is not uncommon to find retail newspaper advertisements that read "Sold in our stock yesterday at . . ." Customers who made a purchase of the identical item within recent days of this ad at a higher price will, to be sure, storm the doors to seek some price-allowance concession, so if customer goodwill is to be retained, the formulation of this markdown policy would have to recognize that the natural reactions of customers will lead to markdowns. Some retailers take these items off sale several days before the advertisement is to appear in order to avoid excessive adjustment markdowns. This is especially true if the sales of the item were extremely heavy several days prior to the effective new sale-price date. If there was very little sales activity on the item prior to the sale date, then the problem would take care of itself.

Within recent years, there has been a tendency by some retailers to eliminate odd-price endings, such as $7.98, and to retail the item for an even-price ending, such as $8.00. The added pennies multiplied by the number of transactions can add substance to the mark-on. However, there are still many retailers who wish to make a strong price appeal and will structure the price lines in odd-price endings. This markdown policy may require the buyer to adjust some of his planned retail prices downward. The extent of the markdown will depend upon the number of items involved in each transaction.

Another markdown determinant will be the merchandising policy of the store—one price or variable price. If haggling or bargaining is allowed, with the buyer or the assistant permitted to make price concessions at their own discretion, then the markdowns will increase. Unwilling to lose a sale, the buyer may be moved to "save the sale" by yielding to the pressure of the customer for a lower price or "no sale." Many buyers have learned that the know-how for this demand by the customer is supplied by the salesperson. Word of mouth will eventually put all of the items in the "haggling" classification.

Merchandise managers will remind their buyers "to buy some markdown merchandise." Embryonic buyers are usually puzzled by this request. The merchandise manager is requesting prestige items that can be used for the windows, interior displays, or fashion shows. Also, some of the items can be displayed in showcases or in stock to give the department a "lift" and to give the customer the impression that the department is not all low-end or dull merchandise. These items will be high priced, different, unusual, and exciting. In all probability, very few of the items will be sold. But the subsequent markdown required to dispose of them will be overshadowed by "the sparks" they generate to provide customer interest and merchandise excitement.

The markdown policy may include provision for the subsidized markdown. This device involves reimbursing the department for all or part of the markdown it has taken, under certain circumstances. A sudden price war between two competitors may find a department caught in the middle with excessive markdowns and with no way to extricate itself. Recognition by the store that the department must stay in the fight at all costs although it was not a willing participant may result in special consideration by the store. A markdown subsidy to offset the total amount of the markdowns may be granted.

In retail operations where all departments are leased, the subsidized markdown may be given to one department by the other departments as compensation for the sale of a "leader item" at cost or less than cost.

The formulation of markdown policies will be influenced by the type of store, the competition, the nature of the clientele, and the merchandising objectives of the store.

[6] Planning of Markdowns

The primary function of a retail operation is to buy and sell merchandise for the purpose of realizing a profit through the satisfaction of consumer wants and needs. To insure the successful completion of this objective, retail stores prepare a merchandise plan or budget of future operations.

Among the more important items planned, and upon which tentative limits are set, are sales, stocks, purchases, turnover, mark-on, gross margin, and markdowns. Markdowns are planned to help the buyer arrive at the proper gross margin. If the retailer plans a mark-on that is designed to cover the expected expenses and the desired profit, but does not take into consideration the possibility of markdowns, the retailer may discover that no profit results from his endeavors. As we have noted, a markdown is an important figure that allows sufficient buying power to realize the planned stock figures. The effect of excessive markdowns is to reduce the gross margin realized.

The object of markdown planning, as far as management is concerned, is that it will encourage the buyer to study his past performances and to analyze the causes of the markdowns for the same period the previous year—and that, more importantly, it will provide the buyer with motivation for improved professionalism. The intrinsic value of planning markdowns, for a given period (usually a month), is to encourage the buyer to make use of the markdown allowance available within the period. In this way, the buyer will search his inventory for items that should be marked down immediately as the month progresses. Thus, if the policy of management does not permit the buyer to "save" or "accumulate" the markdown allowance beyond the planned period, then the need for drastic or excessive markdowns may be avoided. This policy would make it necessary for the buyer to take markdowns as needed from month to month, instead of postponing them until the end of the season. It would be shortsighted for a buyer to refrain from or resist taking needed markdowns that actually exist in stock.

Sales should always reflect the prices at which customers are willing to purchase the items. A low actual markdown figure against the planned figure may indicate that the buyer is too conservative in his approach.

Since retailers realize that one of the best ways to increase profit is through the intelligent planning and use of markdowns, it is for this reason that the markdown figure in the merchandise plan has taken on added importance. If markdowns were not planned, then it is possible that markdown excesses might result from buyers who tend to "push the panic button" too soon when expected sales are not realized immediately.

The extent of the markdown figure to be planned requires the consideration of many factors:

1. An examination of the actual markdown results for the past several years will provide the buyer with a history or experience of the markdown activity for the same period. Fluctuations in the amount of markdowns taken from year to year as revealed by this information can provide valu-

able clues to the buyer as to the reasons for the markdowns and the reasons for any inconsistencies of the operation. It will also serve as a guide for the planning of the markdown amount to be allotted for the same period in the current year.

2. A study of the experiences of other stores can serve to provide comparative figures of other, similar operations. These figures can be obtained from various trade associations, resources, and government bureaus.

3. The planning of the markdown allowance for fashion departments require different considerations than planning markdowns for less volatile departments. An examination of the ready-to-wear fashion departments reveals that they have markdowns ranging from 10 percent to 22.4 percent, while the markdowns for the home furnishing departments ranges from 3.3 percent to 10.2 percent, a considerable difference. Therefore, failure to make sufficient allowance for markdowns in the fashion departments may mean that the stocks will be starved and that there will not be an adequate flow of new merchandise.

4. The current condition of the inventory on hand is an important consideration in setting a markdown allowance. The question of how much inventory has been carried over from the last period of the previous year and the amount of markdowns that will be needed to move the goods must receive serious consideration.

5. The current trend in wholesale prices and competitive prices deserves the attention of the planner. A downward trend in prices may be the signal for a higher markdown allowance than anticipated.

6. Current business conditions generally and the changes in consumer demand for merchandise from a specific

industry requires evaluation in determining the markdown allowance. Consumer affluency may make the need for markdown less likely than at other times.

7. The schedule of the promotional events planned by the store for departments, divisions, or the total store for the coming period may mean that more or less markdowns may have to be taken in the current year over the previous one. This event schedule is usually available in sufficient time to be considered before the markdown figure is determined. An increase in the number or size of these events may result in the need for an increased markdown allowance, particularly if the sale merchandise is taken from regular stock.

The planning of a decrease in the markdown figure for the coming period in comparison to the same period the previous year may be due to several reasons:

1. A shift in calender dates for such important selling periods as Easter. If the Easter holiday fell in March last year but falls in April this year, the planning of the markdown figure will have to be restructured to meet the calendar change.

2. A shift in the dates for a major storewide sales event will cause a change in the planning of the markdown allowance. If the Easter dates last year and this year change, then it is possible that the store may decide to change the date of its storewide spring sale. Naturally, this will affect the planned markdown allotment for each month.

3. The introduction of new techniques and procedures in the control of stocks, such as electronic data-processing equipment, can improve buying and reduce the amount of markdowns required.

It follows, therefore, that the markdown allotment will, in all likelihood, vary from month to month. The variance will depend upon the sales events planned for each month, the time of the year, i.e., if the month is at the end of a selling season or the beginning of a selling season (markdowns are heavier during clearance months); sudden changes in consumer acceptance of fashion; the selling opportunities in the month planned without the need for markdowns to achieve the planned sales figure; heavy carry-over of merchandise from the previous year with drastic changes in the new styles, which make heavier markdowns necessary to dispose of last year's goods; and overbought conditions, which tend to clog the pipelines, thereby preventing the natural ebb and flow of merchandise.

A greater markdown allowance should be planned in those months when the need is greatest. The monthly distribution of the markdown allotment will depend upon the peak selling periods, the kind of merchandise, the type of store, the merchandising policies of the store, and an allowance for the unknown factors or imponderables. The markdown allowance will vary from store to store and as to lines of merchandise. While the markdown allowance is planned, it is not a fixed amount. It is instead a flexible figure designed to meet changing conditions. When properly used, it can be a valuable tool in the merchandising effort.

With the sales for each month planned in the merchandise budget, the markdown allotment for each month can now be allocated. The retailer can approach this procedure in several ways:

1. He can determine the markdown percent the store

wishes to allot for the entire merchandise budget period (six months), expressed in dollars and cents. To illustrate, if the planned sales for the six-month period are $100,000 and the planned markdown percent is 6 percent, then:

$$\text{\$ Markdown} = \text{\$ Planned Sales} \times \text{\% Markdown}$$
$$= \$100,000 \times 6\%$$
$$= \$6,000$$

Based on an evaluation of the factors stated in this chapter, the distribution of the dollar markdown allowance for each month might be allotted as follows:

February	$1,200
March	1,000
April	1,000
May	600
June	500
July	1,700
	$6,000

The distribution of the markdown allowance for each month is based upon the extent of the need for markdowns each month of the planned period. It would be a mistake to allot a strict 6-percent markdown allowance to each month without regard to the exigencies of the month. Since the planned sales for each month may vary, it follows that the markdown percent for each month will vary.

2. By planning the initial mark-on percent and the maintained mark-on percent, the retailer can determine the markdown percent for the merchandise budget period.

3. Once the dollar-planned sales and the dollar-planned markdowns have been established for each month, the buyer can proceed to break down these figures according to the merchandise classifications within the department.

In this way, anticipated sales are apportioned according to the sales contribution expected from each classification. An examination of the peak selling periods of each classification, the selling potential based on style changes, special events, and past experience, will enable the buyer to plan markdowns for each classification within each month.

For example, the breakdown for the men's furnishings department for the month of June might be planned as follows:

Planned Sales: $100,000

Dress shirts	$ 30,000
Sport shirts	40,000
Pajamas	10,000
Neckties	4,000
Underwear	6,000
Miscellaneous—belts, handkerchiefs, jewelry, etc.	10,000
	$100,000

And the markdowns for June might be planned as follows:

Planned Markdowns: $4,000

Dress shirts	$1,000
Sport shirts	1,500
Pajamas	600
Neckties	200
Underwear	200
Miscellaneous—belts, handkerchiefs, jewelry, etc.	500
	$4,000

Through this procedure, the buyer can relate the need for markdowns according to the sales expected from each classification. In addition, each classification will receive the proper attention for markdowns, thereby avoiding the possibility of the bulk of the allotment being improperly apportioned to one or two of the classifications, to the detriment of the others.

It would be correct to state that planning the markdown figure rather than using the hit-or-miss approach makes possible the taking of markdowns at the most advantageous time. And contrary to the opinion of some buyers, the planned markdown figure is not intended as a restriction on the buyer's judgment or activities, but rather to be used as a guide to a profitable operation.

To sum up, retailers plan the markdown allowance for each department in the expectation of certain positive results. Planned markdown amounts, it is hoped, will tend to curb excessive markdowns, will encourage buyers to take the markdown when it should be taken, and will relate the extent of the markdown to progress in sales. And it is hoped above all that intelligent use of the markdown will be made as a means to greater profit.

[7] Markdown Strategies

The obvious purpose of a markdown or reduction in the retail price of an item is to remove the item from stock. If the markdown is too small and does not remove the item from stock, then it is ineffective. The additional markdowns that will be required to finally remove the item from stock may be more costly to the store than anticipated. If the markdown is too large, then the excess markdown becomes a waste and reduces the possibility of realizing a larger gross margin.

The ideal procedure is to determine, as nearly as possible, the true value of the item in the eyes of the customer, and this is best done through a careful reappraisal of the item so as to make a price determination. Seasoned judgment is important in making this determination, which may require a small or a large markdown. The point is that since the customers will not buy the item at the prevailing price, the price must be made more attractive to them. In the eyes of the customers, the new price must represent a "bargain." A correct "bargain" price will provide a greater opportunity to move all or a major part of the goods. Seasoned merchandisers state that the first markdown should move at least 50 percent of the goods from stock.

It is important that merchandise be carefully and intelligently reduced in price if the store is to derive the benefits of the markdown. It is hoped that the attractive new price will result in a quick sale so that the store will have ready cash to purchase fresh, new salable merchandise. Other possible benefits include eliminating the expenses of re-marking, advertising, and window and interior display, and the fact that the remaining stock will take on a cleaner look, quicker. And retailers have learned that a "bargain" price that makes the purchase worthwhile to the customer causes her to overlook the inherent shortcomings of the goods and to concentrate on the "bargain."

The determination of the extent of the markdown involves the consideration of several factors, the most important of which is probably the quantity of the item. It is much easier to dispose of 50 dresses of one style than it is to dispose of 500. The larger the quantity, the greater will be the markdown. It is much more difficult to locate 500 customers who will all be interested in the same style than it is to find 50 interested customers. Therefore, to dispose of 500 dresses of one style may be more expensive, since it may require, in addition to markdowns, an advertisement, a window, and extra selling effort.

The condition of the merchandise is an important influence on the amount of the markdown to be taken. Merchandise that is soiled, damaged, or shopworn suffers in appearance against markdowns of clean inventory. And since customer estimation of the value of the goods is considerably lessened by its condition, a greater markdown will be necessary to move the goods.

The unit value of the goods will be a determinant in how much of a markdown should be taken. The higher the unit price, the greater will have to be the markdown. A customer will expect a generous savings on a $2,000 fur coat if she is to regard it as a "bargain." However, if an item is priced at one dollar, a markdown of 11 cents to 89 cents would constitute a proper savings. Several sample reductions taken from a newspaper read as follows: "Regularly $13.99 to $95.00—Sale $12.59 to $66.50." At the $12.59 price, the markdown percentage is 11.12 percent. At the $66.50 price, the markdown percentage is 42.85 percent.

An examination of newspaper advertisements involving reductions will reveal that markdowns taken on staple goods are smaller than markdowns taken on fashion goods. Staple goods have a constant use and do not become obsolete, as is the case with fashion goods. Markdowns on staple goods are generally taken when there is an overstock and the excess cannot be returned to the vendor. Soiled, damaged, or shopworn staple items are reduced quickly if they cannot be refreshed for selling at their regular prices.

As we have already noted, a delay in taking a markdown when it is needed can cause a greater markdown at a later date. The timing of the markdown then contributes significantly to the extent of the markdown. Overaged merchandise, especially fashion goods, requires a greater markdown if consumer acceptance is to be realized.

Retailers use different approaches to determine the amount of the markdown. Experienced buyers are aware of the old retailing expression handed down by the sages, "The first markdown is the cheapest markdown." The intent of the saying is that if the first markdown is timed correctly and is priced intelligently, there is a greater likelihood that the item will be sold before a second markdown is required. The more modern version of the same saying is, "It only hurts for a little while." Of course, this saying is intended to provide the buyer with the courage to take the markdown action. Ever so many buyers are reluctant to take markdowns.

Different retailers use different approaches to markdown strategies. The first school of thought approaches the markdown in short amounts and continues to take many markdowns until the items are sold—for example, from a retail price of $20 to $19, then $18, and $17, etc., until the items are sold. Those who favor this plan state that it is possible to pick up sales at every price change, and contend that such an approach is legitimate for staple items that will not deteriorate quickly because of fashion, color, or material changes. Those who oppose this approach state that it is not good business to subject the customer to the agony of the clearance process. Further, they contend that, besides the difficulty of inventorying the items, a costly re-marking procedure is involved.

The second school of thought holds that the first markdown should not be more than a stipulated amount decreed by policy, such as $33\frac{1}{3}$ percent of the original price. The second markdown would be 40 percent and the third markdown 50 percent, with no limits on any markdown needed after the third. Thus, if the item is currently retailed at $50, the first markdown price would be $35, the second price $30, the third price $25, and so on. Those who use this procedure state that it prevents the buyer from going overboard on the amount of the markdown planned and that it provides guidelines for an orderly and reasonable disposal of the slow sellers without giving the store away. Flexibility is built into the plan, since special problems can receive special consideration.

The third school of thought believes that the merchandise should be appraised and then priced to answer the question, "At what price will customers remove the item from stock?" This school believes that each item should be appraised for its individual "bargain" price. They do not believe that markdowns should be subjected to the requirements of any plan that does not answer the main question.

The last school of retailers state that all markdowns should be made into the next lowest price full-line. The advantages of this plan are explained fully in Chapter 8, "Timing of Markdowns."

In some retail stores, all four approaches are used in different departments for different types of merchandise at one and the same time. Naturally, the merchandising policies of the store, the type of merchandise, the type of operation, and the urgency of the markdown will be considerations in the decision-making process.

In determining the amount of markdown, retailers are confronted with some interesting mathematical problems.

Problem No. 1. A buyer has planned markdowns amounting to $500. How much of the stock (at retail) can be reduced at 40 percent without exceeding the plan?

Since:

40% of the merchandise to be reduced is equivalent to $500

Therefore:

100% of the merchandise to be reduced is $1,250.

Because:

$$100\% = \frac{\$ \text{ Markdowns}}{\text{Percent of Merchandise}}$$

$$= \frac{\$500}{40\%}$$

= $1,250 (The amount of merchandise which can be re-
duced 40% without exceeding the plan)

Problem No. 2. A markdown of 10 percent was taken on
the original retail value of the inventory. What is the resultant markdown percent to net sales for the period?
Since:

$$
\begin{aligned}
100\% &= \text{Original Retail Value of the Inventory} \\
-10\% &= \text{Markdown Taken} \\
\hline
90\% &= \text{Net Sales}
\end{aligned}
$$

Therefore:

$$\% \text{ Markdown for the Period} = \frac{\% \text{ Markdown Taken}}{\% \text{ Net Sales}}$$

$$= \frac{10\%}{90\%}$$

$$= 11.1\%$$

Problem No. 3. An item is retailed at $10. What will be
the new price if an anticipated price reduction is to be 10
percent of the final selling price?

Since:

$$
\begin{aligned}
100\% &= \text{Final Selling Price} \\
+10\% &= \text{Anticipated Price Reduction} \\
\hline
110\% &= \text{Value of the Original Retail Before the Markdown is} \\
&\quad \text{Taken}
\end{aligned}
$$

Therefore:

$$\%\text{ Markdown in Terms of the Original Retail Price} = \frac{\%\text{Anticipated Price Reduction}}{\%\text{ Value of Original Retail}}$$

$$= \frac{10\%}{110\%}$$
$$= 9.09\%$$

Thus:

$10 = Current Retail Price
9.09% = % Markdown
New $ Retail = $ Current Retail Price × (100% – % Markdowns in Terms of Original Retail)
= $10 × (100% – 9.09%)
= $10 × 91.91%
= $9.09

Problem No. 4. A buyer is planning to sell his stock at a markdown of 8 percent of net sales, or an average of 20 percent off the original retail price. What will be the percent of sales at the marked-down prices?
   Since:

$$\%\text{ Original Retail} = \frac{\%\text{ Markdown}}{\%\text{ Markdown Off Orginal Retail Prices}}$$
$$= \frac{8\%}{20\%}$$
$$= 40\%$$

Therefore:

% Sales at Markdown Prices = % Original Retail – % Markdown
= down 40% – 10%
= 30%

Problem No. 5. A department reported markdowns of 10 percent for a month. The sales report indicated that 30 percent of the total sales were in reduced merchandise. What was the average markdown percent from the original retail taken to move the goods?

Since:

$$100\% = \text{Net Sales}$$
$$10\% = \text{Markdowns}$$
$$30\% = \text{Total Sales in Reduced Merchandise}$$

Then:

% Original Retail of Marked-Down Goods = % Markdowns
+ % Sales in
Reduced Mer-
chandise
$$= 10\% + 30\%$$
$$= 40\%$$

And:

% Markdown of Original Retail $= \dfrac{\% \text{ Markdown}}{\% \text{ Original Retail}}$

$$= \frac{10\%}{40\%}$$
$$= 25\%$$

Problem No. 6. A reduction of 10 percent was taken on an inventory that is completely sold. What was the resultant percent of the markdown?

Since:

$$100\% = \text{Original Retail}$$
$$-10\% = \text{Markdowns}$$
$$\overline{90\% = \text{Net Sales}}$$

Therefore:

$$\% \text{ Markdown of Net Sales} = \frac{\% \text{ Markdown}}{\% \text{ Net Sales}}$$
$$= \frac{10\%}{90\%}$$
$$= 9.09\%$$

Problem No. 7. The prior (aged merchandise) report indicated a retail inventory of $220. It was decided that a markdown representing 10 percent of net sales should be taken. What will be the markdown percent of the original retail value of the inventory?

Since:

$$\begin{array}{rl} 100\% &= \text{Net Sales} \\ +10\% &= \text{Markdown} \\ \hline 110\% &= \text{Original Retail} \end{array}$$

And:

$$\$ \text{ Markdown} = \frac{\$ \text{ Inventory}}{\% \text{ Original Retail}}$$
$$= \frac{\$220}{110\%}$$
$$= \$20$$

Therefore:

$$\% \text{ Markdown Based on Original Retail} = \frac{\$ \text{ Markdown}}{\$ \text{ Original Retail}}$$
$$= \frac{\$20}{\$220}$$
$$= 9.09\%$$

[8] Timing of Markdowns

Many merchants agree that the time to take a markdown is when indications first appear that the customer has lost interest in the item, as indicated by a slowdown in sales. They also agree that the retail price should reflect the price at which the customer is willing to buy the item. If the merchandise did not sell at a higher price, then the price should be reduced while there is still customer interest in the item, albeit at a lower price.

If the markdown is taken as soon as the customer manifests a lack of interest in the item, it is possible to move the merchandise quickly with a minimum of markdown. The customer's loss of interest may be due to the introduction of new styles, a reproduction of existing styles at lower prices, or some revolutionary change in a product. If the markdown is taken as the need arises, after a review of the factors affecting the sale of the item, further markdowns culminating in serious losses can be avoided. Failure to take action at all may result in inventory of an item that will be extremely difficult to dispose of under any circumstances. Merchants who hold to this theory further maintain that, by taking a small markdown as soon as the need for one is apparent, time will be left in the selling season to take additional markdowns as required. Since selling is made easier when the item is still in demand at the right price, the total markdowns taken to clear out the item will be considerably less than if action was delayed or postponed to a future date.

We have learned that markdowns have an effect on the available open-to-buy. If the markdowns are taken as planned, then the open-to-buy is increased, to provide funds to satisfy the planned end-of-month stock. If markdowns are not taken, then the open-to-buy is reduced, providing less money for needed merchandise.

It is true that when markdowns are taken as soon as customer resistance is evidenced, the reduced items are emphasized for quick sale. Many retailers, however, object to reduced merchandise in the same selling area with regular merchandise at original prices, claiming that it attracts bargain hunters, who have a tendency to downgrade the department generally. Regular customers, too, may object to the presence of marked-down merchandise in the department area, since it does not lend itself to a satisfactory shopping atmosphere. Some merchants have stated that the aggressive shopping characteristics of the bargain hunter can make regular customers change their choice of "the place to shop." Their contention is that the principle of Gresham's Law can apply to shoppers as well as it does to money—namely, that "cheap money drives out better money." Similarly, "cheap customers drive out better customers." It is for this reason that such merchants either sell marked-down merchandise away from the department in a "thrift avenue" on the street floor, or transfer it to the basement store.

Those stores that do not favor this policy or approach present a different set of reasons. The better specialty stores state that they would prefer not to tamper with the projected image by littering the store with markdown racks and bargain tables. This does not mean that mark-

downs are not taken when needed. They are. But the emphasis is on serving the needs of regular customers in an
atmosphere that is conducive to buying at original prices
rather than at markdown prices.

Edward A. Filene, one of the great names in retailing,
presented this point of view very intelligently in his book,
The Model Stock Plan:

"Under the model stock plan, markdowns are always made to
the next-lower full-line price. The essence of markdowns under
this plan of operation is to take them soon enough at regular full-
line prices. For instead of setting out our markdowns as a distinct
group of items at a special price to which the customer is drawn
by bargain hunting, we have our marked down merchandise
mingled in with our regular merchandise at the full-line price.
In the full line, the pieces from the next higher full-line price
will certainly shine out as extraordinary values. But if the
customer's preconceived requirements are not met by some of
the marked down items, she has the whole full line to choose from
at the same price.

In this complete assortment, she is almost certain to find it at
lower prices than she can find it in competitor's stores where the
Model Stock Plan is not followed.

But we must not leap to the conclusion that our higher-income
customers during this time will not find in our store as high-
priced goods as they are accustomed to find and as they want.
If they are looking for the almost past season's goods, it is apparent that they will find their accustomed qualities at a much
cheaper price than they expected. And in the de luxe department
and the higher-priced full line they find the early showings of new
goods of the next season. These goods will already be arriving in
sufficient quantities so that we can advertise them—thus increasing our reputation for style leadership while our competitors'
advertisements are still talking about markdowns."[1]

These stores would prefer to project their markdowns

at special semiannual or annual sales. Through the use of this technique, they are able to preserve their basic merchandising and promotional concepts. At the same time, through these special events, they attract those customers who are not able to make their purchases regularly at the store but who care to own merchandise from "the store of their dreams." It is possible that some of these customers may remain as regular customers.

There are other retailers who are reluctant to take markdowns. It is their belief that by postponing the taking of markdowns they will be able to have a gigantic clearance sale quarterly, semiannually, or annually. They hope that the large stocks at great value prices will impress the customers and create the image of a "high-value, low-price" store. In reality, they do not have to go into the market to buy merchandise for these sales, since they are buying their own markdowns.

It does not follow that because the item is not marked down but retained in stock at original prices over an extended period that a longer period of time is provided to sell the item at its original price. While a small quantity of the item may be sold, it is also reasonable to state that a larger markdown may be required at a later date to move the balance of the items.

Retailers generally recognize that a new item has a "span of life." It should arrive in stock at a given time if the full selling opportunity is to be realized. It has a "selling period" or a "selling season," after which it should no longer remain in stock. It is possible, therefore, to give the item a "death date" or "expiration date" when it first arrives in the store. This date can be noted on the price ticket. If the item is still in stock on the "expiration date," then it is time for a markdown. The presumption is that the selling season for this item has ended and that, therefore, action has to be taken to remove it from stock. Thus, buyers can cull their stock for these items on a regular schedule by examining the "expiration date" on the price tickets.

This plan, known as the "automatic markdown," is frowned upon by some retailers on the ground that it is inflexible to changing conditions. From this presentation, it is possible to develop some factors that determine when a markdown should be taken:

1. The rate of sale of the item with reference to the selling season.
2. The store promotional policy with reference to sales, specials, etc.
3. The type of merchandise. Fashion goods cannot be carried over. For this reason, fashion merchandise will show a high markdown. The "span of life" is much shorter than that of a staple item.

Markdowns of staple items are generally taken as soon as the merchandise begins to look shopworn or if an overstocked condition exists. While some retailers practice the policy of carrying over staple merchandise to the next season, the arguments against carrying over staple merchandise are:

1. The money tied up in the inventory is "dead money" and cannot be used to buy fresh, new merchandise.
2. The insurance costs continue.
3. The inventory occupies storage space that could be used for more remunerative purposes.

[1] Edward A. Filene, *The Model Stock Plan* (New York: The Ginn Company, 1967), p. 102.

4. The possibility of breakage, damage, or pilferage exists.

5. Most importantly, a change in customer needs or buying habits, or the obsolescence of the item created by the development of a new item, could create a very serious profit loss.

6. An over-inventoried situation exists, and must be corrected quickly if the selling opportunities for the balance of the season are not to be lost.

7. The condition of the wholesale market has a great bearing on the situation. A market in which prices are declining can devalue the inventory on hand, with the need for markdowns to meet the current prices.

Generally, the promotional calendar of full-line department stores, discount stores, and other operations provide buyers with ample opportunity to fulfill the aims and purposes of the planned markdown figure. Here is a partial list of the promotional activities that provide for disposal of marked-down merchandise while there is still sufficient consumer demand to move it:

1. Seasonal clearances ("Winter Fashion Clearance").
2. Storewide clearance.
3. Annual sale events ("Annual Sweater Sale").
4. Traditional department sales at specific times ("January White Sale").
5. Pre-holiday sales ("Pre-Washington's Birthday Sale").
6. Holiday sales ("Washington's Birthday Sale").
7. Post-holiday sales ("Easter Clearance").
8. Year-end clearances ("Inventory Clearance").
9. Daily Sales ("Monday Magnet").
10. End-of-month sales.

11. Special sale days ("Assistant Buyer's Day").

12. Department sales ("For One Week, Men's Suit Sale").

13. Division sales ("Home Furnishing sale").

14. Semiannual Sales ("Semiannual Ladies Shoe Sale").

15. Manufacturers end-of-season sales ("Hanes Hosiery Sale Week").

16. Traditional post-holiday sales ("Half-Price Sale of Christmas Cards, Wrappings, Ribbons").

17. Box sales ("Buy-by-the-Box" and "1 Shirt $4, 3 for $11").

18. Mid-season sales ("Midwinter Furniture Sale").

19. Department promotions ("Special Purchases or Reduced from Stock").

20. Traditional storewide sales at specific periods during the year ("Opportunity Days").

21. Special purchase sales coupled with reductions from stock ("Manufacturers' Closeout and Reductions from Regular Stock").

22. Transfer or combination sales ("One Item Each of an Entire Man's Wardrobe for One Sale Price").

23. Time sales ("Early Bird," "7 P.M. Sale," "Only 100 Pairs of Curtains, 99 Cents, go on Sale at 9 A.M..").

24. Storewide major event ("Anniversary Sale").

25. Unadvertised specials, which are highlighted by special sign toppers and take-one throwaways.

[9] Minimizing Markdowns

In discussing the reasons for markdowns, it was indicated that no system of merchandising is so perfect as to completely eliminate the need for some markdowns. However, many stores can improve their markdown performance through a careful study and analysis of the reasons for them. A structured program consisting of preventive measures by the merchandise manager, coupled with a post-mortem study to avoid repetitious errors, can do much to minimize markdowns.

In the final analysis, if the buyer purchases what his customers will want, in style, quality, size, color, quantity, and price, and properly retails, displays, and advertises his purchases, then his markdowns will be kept to a minimum.

An examination of the various ways in which markdowns may be minimized by the buyer deserves consideration.

Buying

1. An effective method involves the preparation of a dollar buying plan before purchases are made—by classification, item, color, size, and fabric, to indicate the number

of units to purchase in each classification and subclassification.

2. Broadening the assortment by offering the same item in ten colors may not increase sales, but colors selected to serve the needs of each size and each price range will produce the same sales with a lower inventory and with subsequent lower markdowns.

3. Buyers who maintain meticulous sales records by manufacturer, style, size, color, units sold, and units marked down, from one season to the next, are in possession of a vendor analysis for deciding which vendors should be dropped because the percentage of markdowns are too high.

4. While "want slips" should be evaluated very carefully, they frequently indicate what the customer prefers that is not currently in stock. Buyers who demand "want slips" and who indicate to the sales staff that they are regarded seriously are taking a positive step toward minimizing markdowns.

5. Pretest new items in an effort to get customer interest before a quantity commitment is made. Intelligent buyers who follow the merchandising fundamental, "Taste them and try them before you buy them," have minimized their markdown possibilities.

6. When merchandise is to be purchased for a sale event, the buyer should be just as critical of that selected as he would be of new items. Markdowns can be reduced when the buyer does not adopt the attitude that "it's only for a sale." Once the vendor discovers the indifferent attitude of the buyer toward the sale merchandise, it is more than likely that the markdowns to follow will be greater than if the buyer had examined the merchandise thoroughly.

In addition, in the purchase of special value merchandise, buyers should anticipate the markdowns on the remainders expected to be taken, and provide for this in the initial mark-on on the entire lot of merchandise.

7. Unskilled buyers who make what appears to be a "good deal" at the time of the purchase find it to be a "poor deal" after the sale is over. The most wanted items are quickly sold, leaving a quantity of unwanted items requiring high markdowns.

8. The buyer should reorder promptly. In his zeal to keep his inventory within proper dollar limits, sometimes the buyer fails to reorder good selling merchandise promptly, thus losing the sales he was so anxious to get by running the promotion in the first place.

9. Consideration must be given to the use of own-branded items, or best-selling staple items carried in regular stock, for sale merchandise. The customer realizes substantial savings on a wanted item, the stocks remain clean and balanced, and sales results are assured with satisfactory mark-ons. Markdowns are reduced because there are no remainders.

10. The buyer who places his emphasis on the best sellers in an assortment, and careful purchasing of the fringe items with little or no sales possibilities, limits the markdown potential. The smaller the operation, the more likely it is that the fringe items will be eliminated completely.

11. Control of the processes that result in the accumulation of slow-moving stock, and the establishment of definite procedures for disposing of it on a planned basis, can only result in minimizing the extent of the markdowns.

The best plan for following up slow-selling merchandise

once accumulated is to list it on suitable forms and to follow it up regularly at short intervals until it has been disposed of. The best method of disposal is a reduction to a price low enough to make the merchandise an attractive value, and the application of available markdown to a minimum number of items so as to insure complete disposal of these items, even if the balance of the slow sellers is left temporarily untouched.

12. One of the major benefits to the buyer for concentrating his purchases with a few key or preferred resources is the resultant relationship that makes possible the return of apparent markdown items for credit or exchange.

Some stores frown upon a relationship that shifts the burden of buying judgment to the vendor and relieves the buyer of errors. Other retailers maintain that the purpose of concentrating purchases is to obtain friendly consideration that will make a profitable operation possible.

If there is to be return privilege, such consideration should be established at the outset. There is no question that such an arrangement can lessen the markdown burden.

13. A larger-than-planned inventory requires an immediate analysis of the stock to determine if markdowns are needed to move the broken assortments, old stock, slow-selling items, and inventory lumps. A large inventory figure on the weekly inventory report is a "red ball" and spells danger. Immediate action can save dollars in markdowns.

Selling

1. Discuss the items with the sales staff. Each item must
be sold on its merits and desirability, for without the enthusiastic support of the selling personnel the item is
destined for a markdown.

By talking with his salespeople, the buyer can learn the
reasons for the poor performance of some items. By listen-
ing to his salespeople, he can learn what the customers are
saying about the items in stock, and about the items that
are not in stock and that are needed. A buyer who has a
close rapport with his people on the firing line will achieve
a more effective sales result and fewer markdowns. The
salesperson should be consulted and considered before
and after any purchase is made in the market.

2. A part of the buyer-salesperson rapport includes the
transference, on a regular basis, of merchandise and style
information on new items. Selling from first-hand knowledge provides the salesperson with confidence and assurance. Also, buyers who demonstrate how related items
can be sold find that the average sale increases, while the
markdown decreases.

To talk with, to train, and to teach the sales staff is to
give them a sense of belonging and a feeling of importance
that can only bring rich rewards in the form of greater
sales and lower markdowns.

3. The problem of "lay-aways" as a markdown producer is significant. Too many sales are made on the salesperson's suggestion, "Why not let me hold it for you with a
small deposit? You can always get your money back if you

should change your mind." A definite policy governing lay-aways, including the amount of the deposit and the dates when additional payments are due, will reduce the possibility of excessive "returns to stock" and unnecessary markdowns as a consequence.

Some stores have found that better control of the lay-away operation will result if it is taken out of the buyer's hands and made the responsibility of the credit sales department or controller for follow-up. More lay-aways on credit plans have resulted from this approach.

Employee lay-aways without deposits can create serious markdowns. Those employees who "bury" the items they would like to buy when they are marked down not only remove needed items from stock, but, more seriously, eventually find it necessary to appropriate the item. A strong follow-up procedure by the buyer, assistant, or by the sales manager to ferret out "buried" items, as well as returning to stock "holds" for an undue length of time, will save dollars in markdowns and prevent the development of improper employee attitudes.

4. While many retailers hold that a P.M. or some other form of sales incentive made available to sell slow-moving merchandise is antisocial in its purpose, many buyers have found it to be effective. A P.M. is not classified as a markdown but as a selling expense, differing, therefore, from a markdown in that it does not affect the resultant mark-on. Careful determination of the first markdown timing can make the use of the P.M. unnecessary. To use the P.M. instead of a markdown in all or most instances can lead to skillful manipulations of the inventory by salespeople.

Stockkeeping

1. Experience has indicated that those buyers who place the responsibility for the care and maintenance of the stock on the sales staff, on an assigned basis, minimize the possibility for markdowns.

Stockkeeping is a part of selling, for without good stockkeeping there can be no selling. The responsibility includes: returning unwanted items to stock immediately from the fitting rooms and selling floor so that they can be found when they are needed; returning the item to its proper place; keeping the stock arrangement orderly, according to size or color as planned; requisitioning needed fill-ins; ensuring neatness, cleanliness, and protection to avoid soilage; and informing the buyer when the stock has reached its low point. Protection of the merchandise at night when the store is closed is equally important.

2. Untrained salespeople unknowingly create markdowns by placing new fill-in merchandise in front of the existing merchandise in stock. The old merchandise becomes older and less desirable. Inevitably, markdowns will result if the salespeople are not trained to put the new behind the old.

3. Markdowns result from poor stockkeeping and handling procedures. The pencil or ballpoint pen are dangerous instruments in the hands of a salesperson while demonstrating an item to a customer or when taking a stock count. Exposed carbon paper, dirty counter tops, unclean hands, sharp instruments, and open stamp pads

are only some of the ways in which markdowns can be
created through poor stockkeeping and selling practices.
Lipstick and hair preparations present special problems
in the fitting room, leading to markdowns.

Good stockkeeping keeps markdowns down. Careful
handling avoids damage. And proper protection cuts down
on "as-is" reductions.

Branches

1. The coordination between the main store and the
branches has always been a problem, caused by poor lines
of communication, the branch store's disregard for and
lack of understanding of the need for basic controls when
taking markdowns, delay in taking the markdowns, and
failure to take seriously the recording of the markdowns.

The buyer can contribute to the minimization of markdowns at the branches through better supervision, follow-
up, and patient explanation of the instructions. Markdowns
at the branches can be reduced if the buyer will follow the
simple expedient of putting all markdown instructions in
writing, clearly and legibly. Disastrous errors can be avoided if markdown instructions are not given over the telephone, especially to a worker who is involved in another
assignment at the moment. Regrettably, too many buyers
consider the branches as a nuisance value rather than as a
sales and profit potential.

2. Buyers have learned that the branch store offers an
excellent outlet for disposal of marked-down merchandise

with a minimum of reductions. By grouping all the remainders of special sales for disposal at one branch, the size and color selection is improved and a sufficient quantity is provided to promote the markdown successfully.

3. Buyers who record dates of local events affecting the branch store in their *Merchandising Planbook and Sales Promotion Calendar* (available from NRMA) will find rewarding opportunities to sell off marked-down merchandise with a minimum of reduction.

Chain stores, without a main store and operating from central headquarters, have struggled with the markdown problem for years. Discount operations established without a main or parent store are aware of the importance of minimizing markdowns through proper control procedures and improved merchandising techniques. Now that a trend toward department stores operating without a main or parent store is appearing on the horizon, the need for study in this area is established.

Competition

1. Buyers can minimize the markdowns before purchasing merchandise by inquiring from the vendor what other stores in the trading area will be carrying the item. Important, too, is assurance from the vendor that price protection will be provided to avoid predatory price-cutting.

2. Failure to meet competition may be a potential cause for excessive markdowns at a later date. Meeting the competition head on quickly will make the customer realize

that the competitor's advertised low price is no bargain after all, while postponing the markdown while disputing with the vendor over the competitor's action can be harmful. If the price is returned to its proper point by virtue of the vendor's pressure, the competitor will have gained the advantage. As the fundamental states, "Meet the price first, argue its merits later."

Imagination

1. Someone once said, "A buyer without imagination is like an observatory without a telescope." The buyer who is quick to reach for the markdown pencil as an act of expediency is performing a disservice to the minimizing of markdowns and the pursuit of profit. An objective appraisal of the item to find new avenues of selling opportunities by adding something to the item, or by removing something from it, may make it more acceptable without a markdown. It is quite possible that a slight additional cost may be necessary to effect the change.

Examples of the buyer's use of the imagination processes may be gathered from the following few instances:

- Adding a pompon to slippers to give them a new look.
- Making pillows of fabric remnants.
- Making sets out of individual items.
- Making individual items out of sets.
- Regrouping a quantity of miscellaneous items into new price lines.

It should be realized that effecting a change with an additional cost does not preclude the possibility of an in-creased mark-on.

2. If the item is available in sufficient quantity and lends itself to suggestive selling over the telephone, markdowns can be avoided. Items that do not involve size or elaborate description lend themselves more readily to telephone selling, for example, playing cards, hosiery, men's hand-kerchiefs, and so forth. It may be necessary to make some "push" arrangements with the telephone-operator super-visor to make the effort worthwhile. For too long buyers have overlooked the great sales potential in the ability of store telephone operators to sell unadvertised items.

3. Merchandise that receives a great deal of handling by customers and salespeople; merchandise returned by customers for refund, credit, or exchange; merchandise poorly protected on the selling floor and in the stockroom; and merchandise shipped from the manufacturer without a protective covering will inevitably include a certain number of soiled items. A careful examination of these items may indicate that perhaps a little touching up in the store workroom, or a dry cleaning, will restore a fresh look to the item. A markdown may not be necessary. It is hoped that preventive measures will be introduced in these areas to minimize markdowns.

4. The need for a markdown can be reduced by high-lighting a different slow seller each day. This procedure is most effective when the project becomes departmental and involves all of the selling and nonselling personnel. Each salesperson is given a quota of units to sell rather than a dollar quota, and the merchandise is dramatized with proper display and signs. Intensive, enthusiastic, supportive managerial supervision during the selling day

can provide the dynamite to move a sizable quantity of goods without a markdown. Some of the more innovative buyers have been successful in promoting slow sellers in an area outside of their own departments.

Display

A vast area of avoidable markdowns exists with the items taken by display personnel away from the selling department for use in windows or other areas of the store. Somehow or other, display personnel have always held themselves beyond the need for discipline in conforming to store rules and regulations. Merchandise is literally taken from departments without permission, without consultation, without recording the transaction.

Most stores use the time-worn procedure of a merchandise loan book. The problem of writing the items in the loan book and then checking them off upon return is just too much for the display personnel and for the department. One store tried the technique of charging the items to the display department on a regular salescheck. When the items were returned, a regular credit was issued. Any unreturned merchandise was charged to the display department and credited to the department.

The careless manner in which the items are used in display can lead to markdowns. The use of straight pins, safety pins, glue, bright spotlights, nails, etc., can make these items returned unsalable and suitable only for a markdown. The security department could discover a wealth of markdowns and missing items if they were suddenly, without prior notice, to collect and examine all of the merchandise loan books in use throughout the store.

Only a tough buyer with the nose of a bloodhound and the determination of a bull can protect markdown losses in this area.

Vendors

1. We are all familiar with the quotation, "There are people in business, and business people." Translated into retailing jargon, it says, "If you let your vendors know that you mean business, then you will be respected as a businessman." When you write an order be specific with quantity, colors, sizes, dates, terms, and prices. Fill in all of the spaces, so that no item is left to the judgment of the vendor. If the goods received are not exactly as ordered, it may be necessary to return the whole shipment. Markdowns may be saved if the buyer stops doing business with the manufacturer who disregards the instructions. Once a manufacturer has discovered that he can deliver late, substitute items, disregard the distribution of colors and sizes, and ship in bits and pieces, then he is in control and the order is meaningless.

Buyers who have been through the mill have learned that "the squeaky wheel gets the grease." The buyer who demands, insists, and makes his dissatisfaction clearly known finds that vendor service and adherence to the instructions contained in the order improve considerably.

2. Manufacturers literally steal merchandise from the "softy" buyers to make deliveries to those buyers "who mean business" and who will cancel orders promptly if past due. Ready-to-wear buyers, particularly, know the value of following up orders before they become overdue. It would be useful for the buyer to check with the manufacturer at the time of purchase to see whether he has the materials and can make delivery. If there is any doubt about his ability to deliver when the merchandise is wanted and needed, the buyer may have to buy elsewhere.

3. Of late, too many retailers have abandoned the practice of examining and inspecting every shipment before it is processed. Thus, because difficulties with an item are not discovered until the customer has made the purchase, store expenses are increased and customer goodwill is damaged. Merchandise is generally pushed through the marking process to get it to the floor in a hurry. Even a cursory or spot-check inspection will help to uncover inaccuracies in the manufacturer's shipment and reduce markdowns.

4. The buyer can reduce his markdowns by insisting that the vendor make use of instruction or information tags where misuse by the customer can cause returns for allowances. Buyers who establish a return understanding with vendors for merchandise which has not held up properly in customer use are reducing their markdown potential.

Much has been written and said lately about the lack of quality control at the manufacturer level. Add to this the lack of inspection at the retail level, and the image upon which the retailer has spent millions of dollars can be irreparably damaged. The customer is a customer of the store and not of the manufacturer.

Much can be done to minimize markdowns: through concentration on the proper buying procedures, which are based on a knowledge of the market and the expected consumer demand coupled with a sampling or pretest of the new items; through correct initial pricing of the merchandise based on a studied knowledge of the value of the merchandise and the retails established by competitors; through good advertising based on a review of the reasons for initially making the purchase; through dramatic displays, properly accessorized, and located at the best selling locations, through the application of creative and imaginative ideas to revitalize the sale of the item by reticketing and repackaging the item; and finally through the cooperative effort of the vendor to exchange, accept for return, or provide "markdown money" when a markdown becomes apparent.

None of these actions precludes the need for enthusiatic selling support and good stockkeeping practices.

[10] Control
of Markdowns

An examination of available markdown data reveals a middle-range difference of markdowns reported by various stores within the same sales category for the same merchandise departments by as much as 20 percent.

A segment of this significant difference must be the result of increased efficiency in the control of the markdowns. Effective markdown control involves nearly all of the activities of buying, selling, stockkeeping, and attention to the day-to-day handling of markdown paperwork. The control of markdowns embraces several areas of consideration:

1. A rating or evaluation of the sources of supply.
2. Preparation before the merchandise is purchased.
3. Considerations after the merchandise is in the store.
4. Analysis of the markdowns taken.
5. Control of the mechanical aspects of markdown procedures.

A Rating or Evaluation of the Sources of Supply

While all merchants agree that an operation requires some markdowns, they also agree that the answer to improved profits is a performance that results in a percentage of markdowns that is reasonable and controlled.

Experience has shown that a poor markdown performance starts with poor buying as well as unwise selection. To correct the lack of expertise and professionalism of high markdown buyers, there is need for a plan that would make for better buying. A rating procedure of the sources of supply offers many advantages to the unskilled buyer and many benefits to the store.

1. It eliminates "habit" buying based on imagination.

2. It eliminates buying based on vendor "propositions" rather than on the merits of the product.

3. It spotlights the profit resources as well as those resources that retard the profit potential of the department.

4. It rewards those vendors whose efforts have made a positive contribution to a successful operation and penalizes those vendors who have not made a significant contribution to profit.

5. It adds strength to a "weak" buyer by minimizing his buying efforts in the wrong direction.

6. It serves to increase sales through a decrease in consumer resistance to the items carried, with a subsequent reduction in the cost of selling.

7. It improves customer goodwill through fewer returns to the vendor because of customer dissatisfaction.

8. It serves to strengthen the combined effort of the vendor and the store toward a common goal.

9. It makes it difficult for the buyer to justify doing business with a "poor" performer.

10. It increases net profit through the achievement of the all-important objective—a reduction in the markdown percent.

The advantages of a resource-rating plan will enable the "weak" buyer to prepare a buying plan that will concentrate purchases with vendors who deserve prior consideration. The reciprocal cooperation that will result can only add dollars to the volume and to the profit.

It makes good sense for a buyer, despite personal preferences, to give, objectively, planned consideration to making profitable vendors a part of the buying plan. These vendors have earned the right to priority treatment on the basis of past performance.

The suggested form can be applied to any department or operation, and can be made flexible to serve the needs of individual situations. The major purpose of the rating plan is to make it possible for the buyer to develop a guide for doing business with profitable sources of supply and to eliminate "habit buying." It has the added advantage of providing the buyer with the proper motives to seek out other guides to overcome his weaknesses and to develop his strengths. From management's viewpoint, it will make it more difficult for the buyer to engage in some of the "hanky-panky" that prevails in the marketplace, to the personal gain of the buyer but to the detriment of the business.

Preparation Before the Merchandise Is Purchased

Proper preparation by the buyer before he enters the buying market can determine whether he will commit the store to a profit or to excessive markdowns. This means an alertness to the needs of the store's customers through a careful study of the daily sales reports, unit control records, and want slips, as well as talking to salespeople and visiting the selling floor. Records that will give the buyer information quickly and accurately, with the specifics of the movement of merchandise in each price line by style, color, and size, are important to provide flexibility of action to meet changing conditions.

Preparation for buying should include a knowledge of, and a respect for, the planned figures contained in the merchandising plan, and any adjustment in the figures from week to week. The buyer who maintains and continues close examination of these important indications will avoid buying errors.

The keys then to the correction of buying weaknesses is to know what is needed and what is not needed, what is selling and what is not selling, what should be reordered and what should not be reordered, and what are the new trends and what trends are passing out. Careful analysis of the buying habits of the consumers as revealed by the available records, and persistent attention to this information, can contribute to a control of the extent of markdowns. Knowledgeable buyers read all of the current reliable information regarding their area of merchandise in trade publications and private service reports; they attend meetings, conferences, and trade shows, and make market visits to manufacturers, trade associations, and competitors.

Fortified with a keen knowledge of his own merchandise requirements and a better understanding of the happenings outside of the store, the buyer has done his "homework" to adequately prepare himself for buying.

Considerations After the Merchandise Is in the Store

There is much to be done with the merchandise in the store if the good start achieved through a study of the sources of supply and the preparation of the buying is to be made even better. Regrettably, salespeople like to sell only those items which customers ask for or which are easy to sell. This is especially true if a commission to the salesperson is involved. Regrettably, too, buyers generally pay closer attention to those items that are selling than to those items which do not sell as well.

This mutual characteristic of salesperson and buyer results in the attitude that a markdown is necessary to move merchandise. If this characteristic is permitted to persist, then taking markdowns becomes routine. All of the powers of innovation, imagination, and creativity mentioned in another chapter that should be used to move merchandise without a markdown, are replaced by the habit of finding plausible reasons for marking down merchandise that is not moving as rapidly as it was expected to move.

Merchandise, once in the store, must be "watched" by making certain that the merchandise received is the merchandise bought, through a study of the unit control and sales records. It must be "nursed" through department meetings, the informing of salespeople, good stockkeeping, and proper protection and handling. It must be "nourished" through departmental exposure, by means of drawer and stockroom inspection, departmental display, window display, and advertising. It must be kept "healthy" through enthusiastic selling, suggestive and related selling, sales follow-up, and stock fill-ins. And it must be "sustained" through reorders, the changing of displays, telephone board selling, in-store promotion, the clearing from stock of soiled or damaged merchandise, and continued attention to the selling effort.

Merchandise must be guided through these efforts if an unnecessary markdown is to be averted. The mere buying of merchandise does not ensure the sale of the item at its original price. Unquestionably, these actions involve daily changing of displays, movement of stocks, stock counts, merchandise requisitions, meetings, pep talks, supervision, and a constant awareness of all of the items in stock.

A psychologist once said, "A mother may have five children, four of whom are beautiful beyond compare and one who is really ugly. However, she still has to kiss the ugly one good night just as she does the beautiful ones. It is also her child." Regardless of the fact that an undesirable style or item was purchased, the buyer should remember that every item he buys is deserving of the same attention and consideration. They are, in a sense, all his children. Store managers of chain stores and group managers of branch stores have a tendency to prejudge items, to determine, in advance, which items they like or dislike or which items they think will sell or not sell. When this feeling is visibly made known to the selling personnel (which happens, unfortunately, in too many instances), the item is condemned. Some of this attitude prevails when a new buyer takes over a department. All of the current inventory is condemned, the usual request being for a sizeable markdown to clear out the stocks purchased by the predecessor. Understanding merchandise managers take pains to examine the stock with the new buyer so that a fair and reasonable agreement can be reached on what markdowns should be taken. Hopefully, requested items that were not given markdown approval will receive sympathetic consideration from the buyer.

An Analysis of the Markdowns Taken

As much as markdowns are disliked, every retail operation must have some. But if excessive markdowns are to be avoided, and past mistakes not repeated, then an evaluation and appraisal must be made. This analysis of markdowns is not intended to make the buyer cautious, which could result in timidity, since we recognize that some markdowns must be bought. In fact, if the markdowns are too low, the inference might be drawn that the buyer is not taking the merchandise gamble. We are concerned with markdowns that are too high and that reflect inefficiency.

Our concern, too, as we have said before, is with the improvement of the professionalism of the buyer through an understanding of past errors. Without this knowledge, the buyer will continue to repeat the same mistakes, perpetuating the same markdown condition. A markdown analysis can help the buyer to see his mistakes clearly. Hugh White said, "When you make a mistake, don't look back at it long. Take the reason of the thing into your mind, and then look forward. Mistakes are lessons of wisdom. The past cannot be changed. The future is yet in your power."

The markdown analysis sheet presented in Appendix A is intended as a guide and can be changed to meet individual situations.

Control of the Mechanical Aspects of Markdown Procedures

Markdowns must be controlled if a perpetual record of the retail value of the inventory on hand is to be maintained. Since the extent of the markdowns affects the resultant gross margin, records must be kept of the amount of the markdowns taken.

We have seen that since markdowns are planned, record control of the markdowns are important to the success of the plan. Markdowns play an important role in the available money for open-to-buy. Without markdown records, accurate information would not be available for this statistic. Despite the recognized need for strict control of markdowns and markdown procedures, there are recorded instances where the responsibility for taking and recording markdowns has been based on individual initiative.

The general attitude on the part of most merchants today is that there is a definite need for stringent rules, regulations, and procedures if the loss of possible profit due to reductions is to be controlled. These rules, regulations, and procedures concern themselves with the markdown book, the markdown sheets, the re-marking of price tickets, employee purchases, and allowances to customers.

Markdown Book

1. Only one markdown book should be in use in a given department at a time.

2. The book should be issued to a responsible representative of the department upon the proper presentation of the completed previous book.

3. The markdown book issued to one department should not be loaned out to another department.

4. The book should not be removed from the buyer's office without the consent of a proper authority.

Markdown Sheets

1. Erasures on markdown sheets are not permitted.

2. Lines must be voided and verified by the buyer or by an acceptable signature.

3. Every page in the markdown book should be numbered consecutively and be accounted for.

4. Department numbers should be written correctly and legibly on each markdown sheet.

5. Merchandise should be counted carefully before filling in the quantity on the price-change form. The amount should not be guessed at, but an actual account taken.

6. The buyer or his assistant is to sign the price-change sheet.

7. If the markdown is an additional one, the price-change page number of the previous markdown should be indicated.

8. If it is a markdown cancellation, the price-change page number of the markdown should be indicated.

9. Price-change sheets are to be sent to the controller's office immediately.

10. Price-change sheets are not to be destroyed. If necessary, the entire sheet can be voided, but it must be sent to the controller's office.

Employee Purchases
1. Proper identification should be examined before the employee discount is granted.
2. Unusually large purchases or repeated purchases by the same employee should be questioned and checked out.

Allowances to Customers
1. All decisions on allowances to customers should be made by a designated person or persons.
2. All changes in ticket prices because of an allowance should be made only by the designated persons.
3. The price ticket should be signed.
4. The allowance to the customer should be recorded in the price-change book immediately at the time the allowance is granted. The price-change entry should indicate the salescheck number, register number, and date of the allowance, as well as the authorized signature.

Reducing Losses Through Proper Procedures

The following pertinent information is contained in the booklet "Shortage, The Enemy Within," prepared by the Central Training Department, Personnel Division, in cooperation with the Control Division of Burdine's, Florida.

Marking and Re-Marking

Check that merchandise is marked when required. Do not accept unmarked merchandise unless it is on the approved nonmark list.   .

Check the type of marking. Check that the marking room has used the type of marking which is authorized for your department and that all information you need is included in the price markings.

Check prices for accuracy and legibility against retail. Check that retails on price tickets in each shipment are correct. If prices are incorrect or illegible, be sure proper charge was made to your book stock and return merchandise for re-marking.

Check the department number. Check the department number on each price ticket. Be sure that it is correct. This is most important if the same merchandise is carried in more than one department.

Correct price tickets or signs. Record a price change if the retail agrees with the retail on the marking-room copy of the order and on the invoice and *both are correct.* Reticket the merchandise.

Authorized persons only may re-mark merchandise. The department manager is responsible for re-marking merchandise in accordance with the current re-marking procedure.

Count quantity re-marked. If merchandise is sent to marking room for reticketing because of price change, missing price tickets, etc., check the quantity returned against what you originally sent out. Check that the re-marked price is correct.

Provide signs for nonmarked merchandise. Both the price and the name of the merchandise should be indicated on the sign. The sign should be equally readable by customers and salesperson.

Investigate loose tickets. Investigate all cases of loose tickets without merchandise found in the department.

Check for missing price tickets. Train your salespeople to report cases of missing price tickets or instances where signs are inadequate. Take the necessary steps to have merchandise properly marked.

Check for switched or changed price tickets. Report all discrepancies to the protection department.

Check retail unit. Check that the retail unit is indicated on the price tag or on the sign (*Ex*: $2.95 set of 8).

Multiple prices. Price per each as well as the multiple price should be shown on the price tickets and on the signs. (*Ex*: 2/$5.00 or $2.59 each).

Retail Price Change

Price changes are important records. Price changes are one of the most important documents maintaining book and physical inventory.

Record every markup, markdown, markdown cancellation. Record every price change either upward or downward to prevent discrepancies.

Each page must be accounted for in price-change book.

Every page must be accounted for, as statistical depart- ment maintains a numerical control over the books. *All voids must be sent directly to statistical.*

Before the sale of merchandise, record the price change markdown, markup, markdown cancellation. Retail price- change authorization must be issued by the buyer for price changes on stock merchandise, before the merchandise is re-marked or repriced. Record price changes at the time you change the prices on the merchandise.

Indicate department number correctly and legibly on each change. This is most important if you are supervising more than one department or when the same merchandise is sold in two or more departments.

Record quantity accurately. Count merchandise and re- check the count in quantity on price change.

Markdowns should include all merchandise being marked down. Regardless of the store location (downtown, branch, or Service Building) in case of a promotion, count and mark down all of the stock of the item to be marked down.

Check extensions on price changes. Extend your price changes carefully. Watch out for arithmetic errors—a source of stock discrepancies.

Customer returns. If a customer returns merchandise that is returned to stock at a price different from that at which it was originally sold and credited to the customer, issue a price change to take care of the difference.

Salvaged damaged merchandise. Unsaleable merchandise must be marked out of stock and full retail price entered in the retail price-change book.

Cancel markdowns after sales. If merchandise is sold at the regular price after the markdown sale is complete, issue a price change to cancel the markdown based on the accurate stock count and reticket the merchandise. Cross reference the cancellation to the original markdown. The prices on merchandise in all locations must be the same.

Breakage sheets. In departments selling breakable items, instruct all department personnel, selling and stock, to record broken items immediately on the breakage sheet. At the end of the week, total this sheet, attach a retail price change, and enter the markdown for the full amount.

Adjustment of price. On adjustments, or if we have reduced our price within seven days of the purchase date, the customer may be refunded the difference on an adjustment voucher.

Price changes made at branch stores. Be sure the department manager of the various branch store locations is promptly notified of all price changes on the price change authorization form.

Check prices of new shipments of same merchandise against previous shipments. When a new shipment is marked at a different price from that of previous shipments, issue a price change to mark the old shipment up or down at once (if new merchandise is marked correctly) based on an accurate stock count.

Courtesy of Burdine's, Miami, Florida

Reducing Losses Through Employee Reminders

The following significant information is contained in the booklet "Be Alert," of B. Altman & Co., New York.

Record All Information

according to department procedure. Careless paper work
is a major contributor to shortages. Be responsible:
   Print clearly.
   Use all necessary forms.
   Complete each form correctly.

Handle Merchandise

with care. Stock merchandise properly. Soiled and damaged
stock cannot be sold; it is a loss to the customer and to the
company. Your care of merchandise
   in selling
   in stock
   in transit
will prevent this loss.

Courtesy of B. Altman & Co., New York

[11] Markdowns as a Sales Developer

The very word "markdown" conjures up visions of reduced prices resulting in lost gross margin. To the inexperienced buyer, its raison d'être is solely a device to dispose of bad buying mistakes. To the experienced buyer, it is an effective tool of retail merchandising. Markdown skillfully planned and used can develop new customers, increase sales, and strengthen the store's competitive position in the community.

Thus we learn that the word "markdown" is not a harsh or vulgar word that should present a vision of failure to a buyer. On the contrary, a markdown, when properly used, can be the health serum for a long and prosperous existence. The markdown, then, becomes the adrenalin that races through the store to keep the heart of the business pumping and in a state of good health.

How do retailers make positive uses of the markdown to realize these goals? The answers are interesting and fascinating.

The technique of developing "one-day sales" or "weekend sales" for the purpose of attracting traffic and building sales can be very effective. While the markdown taken will reduce the mark-on on the individual item, the combined sales of regular and reduced goods will produce the desired results. The key to the success of this technique is that the amount of the markdown must be controlled, because uncontrolled markdowns can lead to a "giveaway." Upon completion of the sale, the merchandise is then returned to its original price. To illustrate:

A pair of draperies cost $30 and retail for $50 for a mark-on of 40 percent. The buyer plans to reduce the retail price of the draperies by 20 percent for a one-day sale. How many pairs of draperies will have to be sold at the reduced price to yield the same dollar mark-on?

$$
\begin{array}{lll}
\text{\$ Retail} & = & \$50 \\
-\text{\$ Cost} & = & \underline{\$30} \\
\text{S Mark-On} & = & \$20
\end{array}
$$

If the item is reduced by 20 percent for a one-day sale, then:

$$
\begin{array}{lll}
\text{New \$ Retail} & = & \$40 \\
-\text{ \$ Cost} & = & \underline{\$30} \\
\text{New \$ Mark-On} & = & \$10
\end{array}
$$

A 60-percent increase in sales and twice as many units would have to be sold to result in the same dollar mark-on.

Since:

$$
\begin{array}{ll}
\text{\$ Mark-On on 1 item at \$50} & = \$20 \\
\text{\$ Mark-On on 2 items at \$80 } (2 \times 40) & = \$20
\end{array}
$$

If 100 pairs of draperies were included in the sale and all were sold, the markdown percentage would be:

$$
\begin{array}{lll}
\text{\$ Sales} & = 100 \times \$40 & = \$4,000 \\
\text{\$ Markdown} & = 100 \times \$10 & = \$1,000
\end{array}
$$

Then:

$$\% \text{ Markdown} = \frac{\$ \text{ Markdown}}{\$ \text{ Sales}}$$
$$= \frac{\$1,000}{\$4,000}$$
$$= 25\%$$

The resultant maintained mark-on percent would be:

$$\% \text{ Initial Mark-On} = 40\%$$
$$\% \text{ Markdown} = 25\%$$

Then:

$\%$ Cost of Markdown $= \%$ Markdown $\times \%$ Complement of
the Initial Mark-On
$$= 25\% \times 60\%$$
$$= 15\%$$

And:

$\%$ Maintained Mark-On $=$ Initial Mark-On $- \%$ Cost of
Markdown
$$= 40\% - 15\%$$
$$= 25\%$$

Sales events are used by every type of retail operation in one form or another. Successful sales attract traffic, including new customers, to the store and stimulate the sale of the regular merchandise as well as the sale of reduced or specially purchased merchandise. A fringe benefit from this activity is the reduction in the variable expenses as a result of the increased volume.

Many stores use these events to dispose of reduced seasonal, slow-selling, or broken assortment goods. Other reasons given by retailers for these events are that they help to define the store's character and image, and to bolster the enthusiasm and morale of the personnel.

Retailers have been known to inflate the retail price of a new item when it reaches the store, then, after a short period of time, reduce the retail price to its normal level. This procedure permits the store to advertise the item at a great reduction in price. The bookkeeping of the markdown will depend upon the store and the purpose this procedure serves. If a markdown is taken, it could increase the markdown figure, making planning for the next markdown period difficult. To illustrate:

Fifty rugs are priced to sell at $100 each. The rugs cost $50 each and would ordinarily be retailed for $85. Twenty-five rugs are sold at $100 each. If the buyer wanted to realize a maintained mark-on of 40 percent, what would be the sale price for the remaining 25 rugs?

Since:

$$\$ \text{ Retail at } 40\% \text{ Mark-On} = \frac{\$ \text{ Cost}}{100\% - \% \text{ Mark-On}}$$

$$= \frac{\$5,000}{60\%}$$

$$= \$83.33$$

Therefore:

$$\$ \text{ Total Retail Required} = \$ \text{ Retail} \times \text{ Quantity}$$

$$= \$83.33 \times 50$$

$$= \$4,166.50$$

But:

$$\$ \text{ Sales to date} = \$ \text{ Retail} \times \text{ Quantity}$$

$$= \$100 \times 25$$

$$= \$2,500$$

Therefore:

$ Total Retail Required	$ 4,166.50
$ Sales to Date	− 2,500.00
$ Balance of Sales Required	= $ 1,666.50

Since:

25 rugs are remaining

Then:

$$\frac{\$1,666.50}{25} = \$66.66$$

Each of the 25 remaining rugs can be sold for $66.66, and the buyer will realize a maintained mark-on of 40 percent on all 50 rugs.

To increase the dollar volume of sales and to sell more units of merchandise, stores offer multiple-priced merchandise. The customer gets the benefit of the savings through the purchase of more than one item. For example, "Ladies Hosiery—$1.50 Per Pair, 2 Pairs for $4.00." The marketing value of such a multiple offering is to remove the customer from the hosiery market by satisfying her needs for some time to come. Competition is thereby eliminated for the time being. The operational value lies in a lower selling cost by virtue of a higher sales check. From a trading-up point of view, the average sale is increased.

Mathematically, the markdown can be computed as follows:

Assuming the sale of 5,000 pairs with total sales of

$10,000. Then:

$$\text{\$ Average Retail Price} = \frac{\text{\$ Total Sales}}{\text{Number of Pairs Sold}}$$

$$= \frac{\$10,000}{5,000}$$

$$= \$2$$

And:

$$\begin{array}{l}\text{\$ Retail Per Unit in} \\ \text{Multiple of Three}\end{array} = \frac{\text{\$ Retail of Multiple}}{\text{Number of Multiple}}$$

$$= \frac{\$4.00}{3}$$

$$= \$1.33$$

Therefore:

$ Average Retail Price	$ 2.00
$ Retail Per Unit in Multiple of Three	− 1.33
Difference	$ .67

And:

$ Average Retail Price	$ 2.00
$ Retail Per Pair	− 1.50
Difference	$ .50

Therefore, for every 67 pairs sold at $1.50, 50 would have to be at $1.33.

Since:

$$50 + 67 = 117$$
$\frac{50}{117}$ of 5,000 Pairs = 42.73% Hosiery Sold at $1.33
$\frac{67}{117}$ of 5,000 Pairs = 57.27% Hosiery Sold at $1.50

5,000 Pairs
$\times$ 42.73%
= 2,137 Pairs Sold at $1.33.

Therefore:

$$\$ \text{ Markdown} = \begin{array}{r} \$\ 1.50 \\ -\ 1.33 \\ \hline \$\ \ .17 \end{array}$$

$$2,137 \times .17 = \$363.29$$

Further:

$$\begin{aligned} \% \text{ Markdown} &= \frac{\$ \text{ Markdown}}{\$ \text{ Sales}} \\ &= \frac{\$363.29}{\$10,000.00} \\ &= 3.63\% \end{aligned}$$

An interesting facet of special events is the psychological value of price endings. Consumer behavior studies indicate that odd number-endings, such as 99, 88, etc., suggest a sale price and reductions. Also, when there are many numbers in the price, the consumer finds it easier to remember only the first number.

For example, a television set advertised at the sale price of $199.99 represents to the consumer a price of "one hundred dollars and some change." Stores that recognize this consumer behavior pattern emphasize this characteristic more clearly by making the price $199.88. Some retailers establish price endings as a matter of merchandising policy.

For example, the policy may be stated:

1. Price endings (cents) for regular price goods are to be .50, .75, .95, and .00.
2. Price endings (cents) for sale goods are to be .98 and .99.

3. Price endings (cents) for clearance goods are to be .90.

If every effort has been exerted to move slow-selling goods through greater exposure, greater selling effort, and the possible use of a P.M., then a markdown may be necessary. However, the primary consideration should be to make the markdown serve the best interests of the store in a positive way.

Many merchants recognize that the last two days of the month are likely to be dull days. Marked-down items provide excellent ammunition for attracting bargain hunters through the technique of such events as an "End-of-the-Month Sale," "Red Tag Day," or "Assistant Buyer's Day." These events not only prevent dangerous and undesirable accumulations of poor-selling stock, but they also provide excellent opportunities to dispose of dead stock as well as odds and ends. Merchants agree that these events must be honestly merchandised and vigorously promoted if the store is to attract enthusiastic shoppers, and if the store is to establish a reputation for reliability.

Unwanted and undesirable merchandise at full prices do the store damage all the time. But these same goods, when reduced, can make new friends, provide needed capital, and, most importantly, improve the image of the store in the community. The store, therefore, must adopt a technique that will enable it to exploit the markdown for its own purposes in building a reputation. Some retail organizations have developed such colorful and dramatic events as tent sales, midnight sales, warehouse sales, and twenty-four-hour sales, as a means of promoting both the markdown and the reputation of the store.

When such an event is enthusiastically and intelligently planned, prepared, and executed, the rewards are rich and the benefits are many. Unfortunately, some stores fail to realize their objectives because of half-hearted efforts with weak items that do not represent real bargains. Stores that have been successful have found that the markdowns involved in the effort result in the sale of related items and impulse sales at full mark-on, generated by the excitement of the event and by increased customer traffic. While the main objectives of such sales are clear, some stores support them with special purchases of merchandise on which they realize full mark-on.

Retailers have used "stock sweeteners" to reduce the extent of the markdown, and to generate sales, to good advantage. By adding new, timely, wanted merchandise to a stock of slow-selling goods or to a stock lacking in colors and sizes, the entire stock takes on the look of "newness" and is provided with the needed "lift" that makes it more desirable. The need for a markdown is eliminated, while the opportunities for selling are improved. This technique when accompanied by a change in the location of the merchandise can spark increased sales at regular prices.

Some basic conclusions can be drawn from the techniques applied to using the markdown as a sales producer:

1. Broken assortments should be reduced while the merchandise is current and in demand.

2. Seasonable merchandise should be marked down before the close of the selling season, as the demand lessens.

3. Staple merchandise should be reduced as soon as the control records indicate an overstocked condition, or

when the merchandise takes on a "beat" or "shopworn" look.

4. Opportunities to promote the sale of marked-down merchandise exist in every phase of a season—preseason, early season, peak season, and postseason.

5. Not all items of a range need to be marked down if only some of the colors and sizes are slow sellers. Only those colors and sizes that are slow sellers should receive markdown consideration.

6. Markdowns taken when sales are in an upward swing afford greater opportunities for sales.

7. Markdowns taken during a season will develop sales with greater acceptance than markdowns taken after the season.

An understanding of these considerations based on the merchandising fundamental that "the first markdown is the cheapest markdown" will make the cash registers ring with a minimum of markdowns and a maximum of profit.

[12] The Mathematics of Markdowns

Since some markdowns are necessary and other markdowns are inevitable, an understanding of the computation procedures involving markdowns is basic.

A markdown is a reduction from the original or previous retail price of a unit of merchandise. For example:

Current Retail or Ticket Price	$ 20
New Retail or Ticket Price	− 15
Markdown	$ 5

Until the item of merchandise is sold, the markdown is known as a gross markdown.

Each time the current retail price is reduced in price, the reduction is expressed as a markdown. For example, if the current price of $15 is reduced to $12, then a markdown of $3 is recorded. If subsequently the $12 retail price is reduced to $11, then a further $1 markdown will be taken.

Retail accounting practice (retail method of inventory) requires that the markdown percent be based on the relationship of the dollar markdown taken to the actual selling price. Thus, if a radio enters the stock at $100 (first retail price) and is finally sold for $75 (actual retail price paid by the customer), the percentage of markdown would be recorded as:

$$\% \text{ Markdown} = \frac{\text{Total \$ Markdowns Taken}}{\text{Actual \$ Selling Price}}$$

$$= \frac{\$25}{\$75}$$

$$= \tfrac{1}{3} \text{ or } 33\tfrac{1}{3}\%$$

For the purposes of a one-day sale or for some other sale event, a markdown may be taken. At the completion of the event, if the price of the item is restored to its original price or to some higher price, it is called a markdown cancellation. To illustrate:

Current Retail Price	$25
Markdown	− 5
Sale Price	$20

When the retail price is restored to its original price of $25, the increase of $5 is called a cancellation of markdown or a markdown cancellation.

Markdown cancellations generally are applicable only when they offset markdowns taken within a season. Cancellations of markdowns taken on merchandise that were marked down prior to the beginning of the season are considered as a markup rather than a markdown cancellation. However, some retailers consider cancellations of markdowns as markups regardless of when they are taken.

It is quite possible that the buyer may decide to restore the retail price to a higher figure than the original. Then, any dollar-and-cent addition to the original price would be called an additional markup. To illustrate:

Original Retail Price	$25
Markdown	−5
Sale Price	$20
New Retail Price After Sale	27
	$ 7

Five dollars of the $7 increase would be a markdown cancellation, while $2 of the $7 would be an additional markup.

The difference between the first or original retail price of an item and the actual selling price of the item to the customer (as a result of markdowns and markdown cancellations) is the net markdowns. To illustrate:

100 items originally retailed at $5 = $500
are marked down to $4 (100 × 4)   = − 400
resulting in a markdown of $100

50 items are sold at $4 (50 × 4)   = $200
and the remaining 50 items are restored to the
original retail of $5 (50 × 5)   =   250
resulting in a markdown cancellation of $ 50

The actual amount of markdown taken
(net markdown) is $ 50

Therefore:

Gross Markdowns	$100
− Markdown Cancellations	− 50
= Net Markdowns	$ 50

To find the percentage of markdowns in this transaction:

$$\% \text{ Markdown} = \frac{\$ \text{ Net Markdowns}}{\$ \text{ Actual Sales}}$$
$$= \frac{\$ \ 50}{\$200}$$
$$= 25\%$$

Retail advertisements express the markdown in different ways:

1. As a fraction. For example, "Save $\frac{1}{3}$"—as indicated by the relationship of the markdown of \$5 to the former retail price of \$15.

$$\frac{\$ \ 5}{\$15} = \frac{1}{3} = 33\tfrac{1}{3}\%$$

2. As a percentage. For example, "Save $33\tfrac{1}{3}\%$"—as indicated by the relationship of the markdown of \$5 to the former retail price of \$15, expressed as a percentage.

$$\frac{\$ \ 5}{\$15} = \frac{1}{3} = 33\tfrac{1}{3}\%$$

3. As a dollar-and-cents reduction. For example, "Save \$5"—as indicated by the difference between the former retail price of \$15 and the new retail price of \$10.

Previous Price \$ 15
Sale Price   − 10
Markdown   \$ 5

4. As a percentage of the original or first retail price at which the merchandise was offered for sale, and after several markdowns have been taken. For example, "Save 50% off original retail"—as indicated by the difference

between the first retail price of an item and subsequent markdowns. Say the original price was $50 and markdowns of $10, $10, and $5 were taken, resulting in the current retail price of $25. If the last markdown of $5 was to be expressed as a percentage of the new retail price of $25, we would find:

$$\frac{\$\,5}{\$25} = 20\% \text{ Markdown Percent}$$

If the total markdowns taken, $25 ($10 + $10 + $5), were to be expressed as a percentage of the original or first retail price, $50, we would find:

$$\frac{\$25}{\$50} = 50\% \text{ Markdown Percent}$$

It would therefore appear to be more expedient for the retailer to express the percentage of markdown in a manner that would reflect the greatest savings to his customers.

5. As a percentage of the current retail price, where the markdown is the first reduction in the retail price of the item. For example, "Save $33\frac{1}{3}\%$ off the regular price"—as indicated by the relationship of the markdown to the regular or first retail price.

Regular Price	$ 20
New Retail Price After First Markdown	− 15
Markdown	$ 5

$$\frac{\$\,5}{\$15} = 33\frac{1}{3}\%$$

6. As a general statement, without indicating the extent of the reduction. For example, "Now—tremendous reductions in all departments."

With these considerations in mind, an examination of the advertising typical of retailers indicates the use of the following formulas to express markdown savings to the consumer:

- —— to —— off.
- Sold in stock $ ——, now pay only $ ——.
- ——% off.
- Sale $ ——, now pay only $ ——.
- ——% off regular prices.
- —— to —— off regular prices.
- Sale $ ——. Regularly $ ——, now $ ——.
- Sale $ ——. Originally $ ——, now $ ——.
- —— to —— off original prices.
- Reduced ——% to ——% off.
- Save up to ——%.
- Sale $ ——. Sold earlier this season for $ ——.
- Save $ —— to $ ——. Regularly $——.
- Sold in our stock $ ——, now pay only $ ——.
- Were $ ——. Now $ ——.
- Formerly $——, now $——.
- Now $ ——. Regularly $ ——.

Other terminology used by retailers is intended to reflect a savings to the consumer from the usual retail price of the item but not as a result of a markdown:

- Usually $ ——. Now $ ——.
- Made to sell for $ ——, now $ ——.
- Sale-priced at only $ ——.
- Value! $ ——.
- Only $ ——.
- Fantastic buy at $ ——.
- Scoop! $ ——.
- Manufacturer's closeout $ ——.

Although the markdown percent is determined by relating the dollar markdown to the actual dollar sales, the resultant answer must be adjusted to represent the true markdown or actual loss.

If we assume that a sweater is purchased from a vendor for $6 and is retailed to sell for $10, the difference or mark-on is $4. Let us suppose that someone shoplifts the sweater. What actual loss did the store sustain? Obviously, since the store's merchandise investment in the sweater is only $6, then the actual loss to the store is $6. The mark-on does not represent a loss since it is an amount that the store had "hoped" to realize.

If this concept is applied to markdowns, then it can be realized that the loss to the store caused by the markdown is not the entire markdown, but only the cost value of the markdown. More specifically, if an item that bears a cost of $6 and a retail price of $10 is reduced to $8, the markdown is $2. However, the $2 markdown consists of two elements—the hoped-for mark-on and the cost of the merchandise. To determine the "true" loss caused by the markdown, it would be necessary to reduce the retail value of the markdown ($2) to its cost value. To illustrate:

$$\% \text{ Initial Mark-On} = \frac{\$ \text{ Mark-On}}{\$ \text{ Retail Price}}$$
$$= \frac{\$ 4}{\$ 10}$$
$$= 40\%$$

Then:

$$\$ \text{ Cost of Markdown} = \$ \text{ Markdown} \times \% \text{ Complement of Initial Mark-On}$$
$$= \$ 2 \times 60\%$$
$$= \$ 1.20$$

which represents the true value of the markdown.

Merchandise personnel must be concerned with the amount of markdowns that can be taken during a period and still achieve the desired maintained mark-on. There is little point to a period of intense activity without some tangible result or reward for the effort. To illustrate, a buyer has the following planned figures:

Planned $ Sales	$100,000
Planned % Initial Mark-On	40%
Planned % Maintained Mark-On	34%

To date:

$ Sales	$ 75,000
$ Markdowns	$ 7,000

What additional markdowns may be taken during the period and still achieve the desired maintained mark-on of 34 percent?

$$\% \text{ Cost of Markdown} = \% \text{ Initial Mark-On} - \% \text{ Maintained Mark-On}$$
$$= 40\% - 34\%$$
$$= 6\%$$

$$\% \text{ Retail Markdown} = \frac{\% \text{ Cost Markdown}}{\text{Complement } \% \text{ Initial Mark-On}}$$
$$= \frac{6\%}{60\%}$$
$$= 10\%$$

Then:

$$\$ \text{ Total Markdowns Allowable} = \$ \text{ Planned Sales} \times \% \text{ Markdown}$$
$$= \$100,000 \times 10\%$$
$$= \$ 10,000$$

Since $7,000 in markdowns has already been taken, then:

$ Total Markdowns Allowable $10,000
$ Markdowns Taken to Date   − 7,000
Balance of Available Markdowns $ 3,000

Therefore, $3,000 is available for markdowns for the balance of the period. Further:

$ Planned Sales $100,000
$ Sales to Date   − 75,000
Balance of Planned Sales $ 25,000

Therefore, the planned sales for the balance of the period is $25,000. Finally, the markdown percent for the balance of the period is:

$$\% \text{ Markdown} = \frac{\$ \text{ Markdown}}{\$ \text{ Net Sales}}$$
$$= \frac{\$ \ 3,000}{25,000}$$
$$= 12\%$$

At various times a store will advertise a reduction of "x" percent and indicate the new price. However, the advertisement does not indicate the original price. If the merchandise manager were to suggest that the buyer reduce the price of an item that should represent "x" percent of the original retail, the buyer could determine the amount of the original price. To illustrate:

The new selling price of an item is to be $1.25. The markdown is to be 20 percent. What was the original selling price?

$$\$1.25 = 100\%$$

after a 20% markdown; therefore, the original retail before

the markdown was 120%. Then:

$Original Price = $ New Retail Price × % Original Retail
                = $1.25 × 120%
                = $1.50

We have learned that while the dollar markdown is taken on the original or last price of the item, the markdown percent indicated on the various reports issued from the controller's office is based on the net sales or the price paid by the customer. To illustrate:

A markdown of 15 percent was taken on the original retail price of an item. What markdown percent will be reported by the controller?

Assume:

Original Price of the Item	$100
Markdown of 15%	− 15
Net Sales or Actual Selling Price	$ 85

Then:

$$\% \text{ Markdown} = \frac{\$ \text{ Markdown}}{\$ \text{ Actual Selling Price}}$$

$$= \frac{\$15}{\$85}$$

$$= 17.64\%$$

The problem of disposing of current merchandise at a reasonable markdown price presents a problem to the buyer. For example:

An item is currently in stock at the original price of $110. The buyer wishes to reduce the retail price of the item so that the percent of markdown will represent a markdown of 10 percent of the selling price. To what price should the item be marked?

Since the actual selling price or net sales is represented by 100 percent, then:

$$\% \text{ Original Retail} = \text{Selling Price} + \% \text{ Markdown}$$
$$= 100\% + 10\%$$
$$= 110\%$$

But the original price is $110 and :

$$110\% = \$110$$

To determine the dollar value of the markdown:

$$\frac{\$110}{110\%} = \$1 \text{ or } 1\%$$

But the buyer desires to take a markdown of 10 percent. Therefore, the markdown will be:

$$\$1 \times 10\% \text{ or } \$10$$

The new price should be:

$$\$110 - \$10 = \$100$$

In this illustration, the markdown percent based on the original retail is:

$$= \frac{\$ \text{ Markdown}}{\$ \text{ Original Retail}}$$
$$= \frac{\$10}{\$110}$$
$$= 9.09\%$$

While the markdown percent based on the actual selling price is:

$$= \frac{\$ \text{ Markdown}}{\$ \text{ Selling Price}}$$
$$= \frac{\$10}{\$100}$$
$$= 10\%$$

A store wishes to close out a classification of merchandise at markdown prices to reflect a 10 percent markdown at the close-out or sale prices. It is the aim of the store that the markdowns should not be more than 25 percent off the original prices. What should be the percent of sales at the marked-down prices?

Assume the total sales to be $100. Then:

$$\$ \text{ Markdown} = \% \text{ Markdown at Sale Prices} \times \text{Total } \$ \text{ Sales}$$
$$= 10\% \times \$100$$
$$= \$10$$

Then:

$$\$ \text{ Original Retail} = \frac{\$ \text{ Markdown}}{\% \text{ Markdown Off Original Retail}}$$
$$= \frac{\$10}{25\%}$$
$$= \$40$$

Therefore:

$$\$ \text{ Sales at Reduced Prices} = \$ \text{ Original Retail} - \$ \text{ Markdowns}$$
$$= \$40 - \$10$$
$$= \$30$$

However:

$$\% \text{ Sales at Markdown Prices} = \frac{\$ \text{ Sales at Markdown Prices}}{\$ \text{ Total Sales}}$$
$$= \frac{\$30}{\$100}$$
$$= 30\%$$

When a markdown is contemplated, the buyer must realize the extra selling effort required to offset the loss caused by the markdown. Since the purpose of a markdown may be to attract more traffic, it is reasonable to expect that the increased traffic will result in increased sales, thereby compensating for the markdown. To illustrate:

An item is purchased for $6 and retailed at $10. It is planned to reduce the retail price of the item by 20 percent to $8 for sale purposes. What percentage increase in unit sales will be necessary to produce the same dollar mark-on as when the retail price was $10?
Since the cost is $6, the mark-on would be:

Cost	Retail	Mark-On
$6	$10	$4
$6	$ 8	$2

It follows, therefore, that 2 units at $8 must be sold to equal the mark-on of 1 unit at $10, or a 100 percent increase in sales.

2 Units at $2 Mark-On = $4
1 Unit at $4 Mark-On = $4

If the buyer should decide to reduce the $10 retail price of the item by 30 percent to $7, then the increase in needed unit sales becomes increasingly greater. To illustrate:
Since the cost is $6, the mark-on would be:

Cost	Retail	Mark-On
$6	$10	$4
$6	$ 7	$1

Then, 4 units at $7 must be sold to equal the mark-on of 1 unit at $10, or a 300 percent increase in sales.

4 Units × $1 Mark-On = $4
1 Unit × $4 Mark-On = $4

Many buyers experience difficulty maintaining a running record of the extent of the dollar markdowns that remain to be taken for a period. If a store informed the buyer that he could plan to take a 10 percent markdown of his net sales, it would be necessary for the buyer to be able to figure the dollar markdown taken and the dollar markdown allowable for the balance of the period. To illustrate:

A buyer has planned sales of $50,000 for the month of July, with a 10 percent allowable markdown. The first week his net sales were $12,000, with recorded markdowns of $1,500. The second week his net sales were $14,500, with recorded markdowns of $2,000. Based on his actual sales, what dollar markdown may be taken for the balance of the period?

Sales to Date	Markdowns to Date
$12,000	$ 1,500
+14,500	+ 2,000
$26,500	$ 3,500

It will be noted that, from the figures to date, sales are 5 percent ahead of plan. However, markdowns are being taken at a higher percentage than planned.

$$\% \text{ Markdown} = \frac{\$ \text{ Markdown}}{\$ \text{ Net Sales}}$$
$$= \frac{\$ \ 3,500}{\$26,500}$$
$$= 13.21\%$$

If it is assumed that sales will continue at the present pace, then:

Planned Sales	$50,000
5% Ahead of Plan	+ 2,500
New Planned Sales	$52,500

Since markdowns are planned at 10 percent of sales, then:

$$\$ \text{ Markdowns} = \text{ Planned Sales} \times \% \text{ Markdown}$$
$$= \$52,500 \times 10\%$$
$$= \$5,250$$

Since:

Available $ Markdown	$ 5,250
Markdowns Taken to Date	− 3,500
Balance of Available Markdowns	$ 1,750

$1,750 represents the available markdowns for the balance of the period.

Controlling Markdowns to Achieve a Mark-On

We have seen that the relationship of the markdown to the maintained mark-on is significant. Buyers must be mindful of the effect of planned sale prices on the mark-on. Similarly, an understanding of this relationship will enable the buyer to make, intelligently, a profitable decision. To illustrate:

A buyer purchased 500 sweaters at $10.00 each to retail at $17.50 each. At the end of four weeks the control records indicated sales of 400 sweaters. He plans to reduce the remaining sweaters for a Founders' Day sale. What should the new retail price of the sweaters be, after the markdown is taken, if a 40-percent maintained mark-on is desired on the 500 sweaters?

$$\text{\$ Total Cost} = \text{Number of Sweaters} \times \text{\$ Cost of Each Sweater}$$
$$= 500 \times \$10$$
$$= \$5,000$$

$$\text{\$ Retail at } 40\% = \frac{\text{\$ Total Cost}}{\text{Complement of \% Maintained Mark-On}}$$
$$= \frac{\$5,000}{60\%}$$
$$= \$8,333.33$$

Since 400 sweaters have been sold at $17.50 each, then:

$ Sales to Date = No. of Sweaters Sold × $ Retail Price
                = 400 × $17.50
                = $7,000.00

$ Retail Sales Required $ 8,333.33
$ Retail Sales to Date   − 7,000.00
Balance of Sales Required $ 1,333.33

But 100 sweaters are remaining. Therefore:

$$\text{New \$ Retail Price} = \frac{\text{\$ Additional Sales Required}}{\text{No. of Sweaters Remaining}}$$

$$= \frac{\$1,333.33}{100}$$

$$= \$13.33$$

Current Retail Price $17.50
New Retail Price   −13.33
Markdown on Each Sweater $ 4.17

The total dollar markdown to be taken is:

100 Sweaters × $4.17 = $417.00

The 100 remaining sweaters can be reduced from $17.50 to $13.33, and if the 100 sweaters are sold, the buyer will realize a mark-on of 40 percent on the entire 500 sweaters.

With this basic understanding of the mathematics of markdowns, the reader will find these additional markdown situations interesting:

Problem: The desired maintained mark-on is 30 percent. The planned initial mark-on is 35 percent. What is the maximum markdown that can be taken?

Solution

$ Cost of Markdowns = % Initial Mark-On
$$- \text{% Maintained Mark-On}$$
$$= 35\% - 30\%$$
$$= 5\%$$

Then:

$$\text{% Markdown at Retail} = \frac{\text{% Cost of Markdown}}{\text{% Complement of Initial Mark-On}}$$
$$= \frac{5\%}{65\%}$$
$$= 7.69\%$$

Problem: In a given department the records indicate that the markdown to date amounted to 5 percent while 25% of the merchandise sold was reduced. What was the markdown percent taken on the original value of the inventory?

Solution

$$\text{Net Sales} = \$100$$

Then:

$ Marked-Down Merchandise = $ Sales
$$\times \text{% of Merchandise}$$
$$\text{Sold at Reduced Prices}$$
$$= \$100 \times 25\%$$
$$= \$25$$

And:

$ Markdowns = $ Sales × % Markdown
$$= \$100 \times 5\%$$
$$= \$5$$

But:

$ Original Price of Merchandise = $ Net Sales + $ Markdown
$$= \$25 + \$5$$
$$= \$30$$

Then:

$$\% \text{ Markdown of Original Price} = \frac{\$ \text{ Markdown}}{\$ \text{ Original Price}}$$
$$= \frac{\$ 5}{\$30}$$
$$= 13.33\%$$

Problem: The planned sales for February amounted to $50,000, while the planned markdowns for February were 10 percent. Actual sales for the first three weeks were $40,000, and actual markdowns for the first three weeks equaled 12 percent. How much in additional markdowns can be taken for the last week of the month?

Solution

	Sales	% Markdown	$ Markdown
Planned	$50,000 ×	10%	= $5,000
Actual	$40,000 ×	12%	= −$4,800
Remaining Available Markdowns			$ 200

Problem: The current retail price of an item is $10. An 8-percent reduction of the new or reduced selling price is anticipated. What percentage of markdown of the original price of $10 may be taken and what will be the new price?

Solution

$$\text{New or Reduced Selling Price} = 100\%$$
$$\text{Anticipated Markdown} = 8\%$$

Therefore:

$$\% \text{ Markdown of Original Retail} = \frac{\% \text{ Markdown}}{\$ \text{ New Price} + \% \text{ Markdown}}$$
$$= \frac{8\%}{108\%}$$
$$= 7.40\%$$

Since:

$$\$ \text{ Markdown} = \$ \text{ Current Retail} \times \% \text{ Markdown}$$
$$= \$10 \times 7.40\%$$
$$= .74 \text{ (cents)}$$

Then:

$$\$ \text{ New Selling Price} = \$ \text{ Current Price} - \$ \text{ Markdown}$$
$$= \$10.00 - .74$$
$$= \$9.26$$

Problem: What will be the maintained mark-on in a department with a planned initial mark-on of 42 percent and an actual markdown of 8 percent?

Solution

$$\% \text{ Cost of Markdowns} = \% \text{ Retail Markdowns} \times \% \text{ Complement of Initial Mark-On}$$
$$= 8\% \times 58\%$$
$$= 4.64\%$$

Thus:

% Maintained Mark-On = % Initial Mark-On = % Cost of
$$\text{Markdowns}$$
% Maintained Mark-On = 42% − 4.64%
$$= 37.36\%$$

Problem: The new selling price of an item is $12.50 after a markdown of 20 percent has been taken. What was the original selling price?

Solution

$$\text{Net New Selling Price} = 100\%$$

Then:

Original Retail Price = % New Selling Price +
$$\% \text{ Markdown}$$
$$= 100\% + 20\%$$
$$= 120\%$$

Therefore:

$ Original Retail = $ New Selling Price × % Original
$$\text{Retail Price}$$
$$= \$12.50 \times 120\%$$
$$= \$15.00$$

A Ready Reference Chart

Showing the resultant maintained mark-on when a mark-down is applied to the initial mark-on percent.

INITIAL MARK-ON PERCENT	MARKDOWN PERCENT							
	3%	4%	5%	6%	7%	8%	9%	10%
25%	22.75	22.00	21.25	20.50	19.75	19.00	18.25	17.50
26%	23.78	23.04	22.30	21.56	20.82	20.08	19.34	18.60
27%	24.81	24.08	23.35	22.62	21.89	21.16	20.43	19.70
28%	25.84	25.12	24.40	23.68	22.96	22.24	21.52	20.80
29%	26.87	26.16	25.45	24.74	24.03	23.32	22.61	22.90
30%	27.90	27.20	26.50	25.80	25.10	24.40	23.70	23.00
31%	28.93	28.24	27.55	26.86	26.17	25.48	24.79	24.10
32%	29.96	29.28	28.60	27.92	27.24	26.56	25.88	25.20
33%	30.99	30.32	29.65	28.98	28.31	27.64	26.97	26.30
34%	32.02	31.36	30.70	30.04	29.38	28.72	28.06	27.40
35%	33.05	32.40	31.75	31.10	30.45	29.80	29.15	28.50
36%	34.08	33.44	32.80	32.16	31.52	30.88	30.24	29.60
37%	35.11	34.48	33.85	33.22	32.59	31.96	31.33	30.70
38%	36.14	35.52	34.90	34.28	33.66	33.04	32.42	31.80
39%	37.17	36.56	35.95	35.34	34.73	34.12	33.51	32.90
40%	38.20	37.60	37.00	36.40	35.80	35.20	34.60	34.00
41%	39.23	38.64	38.05	37.46	36.87	36.28	35.69	35.10
42%	40.26	39.68	39.10	38.52	37.94	37.36	36.78	36.20
43%	41.29	40.72	40.15	39.58	39.01	38.44	37.87	37.30
44%	42.32	41.76	41.20	40.64	40.08	39.52	38.96	38.40
45%	43.35	42.80	42.25	41.70	41.15	40.60	40.05	39.50
46%	44.38	43.84	43.30	42.76	42.22	41.68	41.14	40.60
47%	45.41	44.88	44.35	43.82	43.29	42.76	42.23	41.70
48%	46.44	45.92	45.40	44.88	44.36	43.84	43.32	42.80
49%	47.47	46.96	46.45	45.94	45.43	44.92	44.41	43.90
50%	48.50	48.00	47.50	47.00	46.50	46.00	45.50	45.00

[13] Price-Ticket Policies

Price changes may be required to raise the existing price of an item or to lower it. If there is no movement of price, either upward or downward, then only a re-marking procedure is involved in the completion of the operation.

There is no general agreement among retailers on the proper approach to use to alter the existing price on a price ticket. There is, however, general agreement that when the existing price is to be raised, the price change should be so effected that the former price will not be available to the customer. Care must be exercised to make sure that careless price-changing practices, which will discredit the store with the customers, do not prevail. Doubt, suspicion, and criticism will occupy the mind of the customer if the store fails to remove the previous lower price completely. Placing a new gummed price sticker indicating a higher price over a gummed price sticker indicating a lower one is the kind of careless price-changing practice that, when discovered by a customer and passed on to other customers, can earn the store a doubtful reputation.

The disagreement among retailers concerns several approaches to price changes:

1. Should both the former price and the markdown price(s) be shown on the price ticket?

2. How many markdown prices should be shown on a price ticket?

3. When a markdown is taken, should a new price ticket indicating only the markdown price replace the existing price ticket?

4. Should there be a uniform procedure for indicating the marked-down price on a price ticket? Specifically, machine-printed prices, the use of special-type marking pencils, the use of ink, or the use of a colored crayon pencil.

5. Should the use of some other form of markdown identification be permitted without indicating the actual new marked-down price on the price ticket? Specifically, the attachment of a special tag to an item during a sale period indicating that the particular item is available to the customer at a reduction of "x" percent.

Retailers and customers agree, however, on several points involving price tickets, whether or not a price change has been taken. The price tickets should be neat and legible to remove any doubt or confusion, and the markings on them made permanent to withstand constant handling. The price numbers should be clean and open to remove any doubt as to the correctness of the numbers, and some special marking device should be used to prevent price changes from being made on the ticket by un-authorized personnel. Price-changing practices should be uniform, to remove any suspicion in the customer's mind that the new price is not the officially changed price. The new price must not be recorded on the price ticket in such a way as to damage the merchandise, and should be recorded in a manner that will clearly indicate that it is the last price, and that the other prices on the price ticket are canceled prices.

The need for established policies regarding price changes on price tickets is heightened by the realization of the many and varied forms of price tickets that retail stores use—pin, string, sew-on, and slip-fold, gummed labels and button tickets; rubber stamps, grease-pencils, and crayons, as well as bulk markings and no markings.

Many of the problems relating to the bad practices of price changing can be traced to two operational procedures:

1. Under pressure from the merchandising division, the management may permit the department to change prices on price tickets without direction or supervision from the marking division, an action caused by the need for more merchandise immediately during a sale period.

Since it is important to take advantage of the strong customer response as a result of an advertised sale, it is understandable that the merchandising division does not want to lose the advantage by processing a price change through the normal channels; time is of the essence if maximum sales are to be realized while customer traffic is in the store. As a result, hasty price changes are made by untrained marking personnel. Working under this kind of pressure and charged with the urgency of the moment, all of the established store procedures and policies regarding price changes can easily be violated.

2. It is recognized that price changing is expensive, and also that it is generally more costly than the original marking of the merchandise. Therefore some stores may permit the department to have its own marking machine,

blank price tickets, and marking equipment. The buyer may be permitted to record, change, and verify his own price changes by making use of his own personnel. While this procedure may result in payroll savings for the store, it may also result in greater losses to the store through increased stock shortages and price-ticket manipulations.

A closer examination of the procedures listed on page 142 will provide greater insights into the reasons for the different approaches by retailers in establishing price-ticket policies.

The retailers whose policies require a price change that show both the former price and the new markdown price believe in the retailing fundamental that "the world loves a bargain." There are others who state that by showing the markdown the retailer is really making the customer ask, "What's wrong with the merchandise?" But there are many customers who are classified as "bargain hunters," just as there are many customers who are willing to be convinced that the intended purchase represents a true saving.

Experience indicates that, when the markdown is not shown on the price ticket and the salesperson indicates that the item has been marked down, the customer's next question is certain to be, "What was it marked down from?" Retailers who insist upon showing the former price and the new marked-down price state that customers want to know when an item is reduced in price as well as the extent of the reduction. To act otherwise would be a refusal to recognize a basic customer shopping attitude. By indicating the markdown, buying and selling are made easier. Another advantage, retailers state, is that revealing the markdown makes possible the highlighting of the reduced merchandise for quick sale. In this way the need for further markdowns is diminished, thereby reducing the possibility of greater losses.

The question of how many markdown prices should be permitted on a price ticket depends upon the size of the ticket, the availability of space on the price ticket, the nature of the merchandise, and the policy of the store.

Some stores maintain that, regardless of the price ticket, not more than two markdown prices shall appear on the ticket at any time. If a third markdown is necessary, then a new price ticket is to be put on the merchandise, one that would indicate only the original or first retail price, and the last or newest markdown price, thereby reducing misunderstandings and losses. Other retailers permit an unlimited number of prices on a price ticket, even though this too often invites misreadings, unnecessary losses, and disagreement with customers, who might insist that the salesperson is reading the price incorrectly. Such policy usually leads to prices being written horizontally, vertically, and over each other on the price ticket, making deciphering difficult. Considerable losses can result especially at the check-out counter, where an inexperienced cashier, under pressure to service a long line of customers, may not have the time to scrutinize the price ticket carefully.

Several stores prefer the practice of removing the price ticket and replacing it with a new one that indicates only the new marked-down price. They maintain that soiled, much-handled price tickets give merchandise an old look, and that new tickets will give it a fresh, new look. They state further that new ticketing removes the general atmosphere of bargain-hunting, thereby maintaining the status of the other merchandise in the area that has not been reduced. Mainly, they insist that greater markdown control is made possible through the application of this policy. This policy of new price tickets containing only one price is prevalent in the ready-to-wear classifications of merchandise. It is recognized that, due to labor and supplies considerations, this procedure is more costly to effect, since it requires more time to replace tickets than it does to indicate a new price on the same ticket.

Knowledgeable merchants agree that the marking implement should be of a type that would preclude imitation or duplication by customers or employees. This would eliminate ballpoint pens, pen and ink, pencils (both lead and colors), or any other writing implement easily obtainable by customers or employees. Machine-printed numbers, special indelible markdown pencils, or special color crayons are more desirable for making changes on price tickets.

In some departments of retail stores, such as furs, better jewelry, furniture, and rugs, handwritten tickets are used. Handwritten tickets are more desirable when merchandise is sold from sample or in those instances where the nature of the merchandise requires a more dignified, personal approach. Such a ticket gives an item an aura of prestige, making the customer feel that it is the only one of its kind. While some contend that handwritten tickets make dishonesty easier to achieve, the advantages seem to outweigh the disadvantages to those retailers who use this procedure.

For "one day only" sales, some stores use the procedure

of putting a color tag on the item to indicate the new marked-down price, as "20% Off" or "Today Only, $35.88," without actually recording a price change. The argument in favor of this procedure is that it saves time and money, since the price tickets do not have to be changed twice—once when the markdown is taken and then to restore the price. Further, it takes the pressure off the marking division, which would have to effect these two changes quickly. And merchandise men contend that a color tag on an item for a one-day sale provides the drama and excitement that motivate the customer to purchase. As the sale of the item is made, the cashier staples the color tag to the sales check and changes the price ticket to the markdown price. At the end of the selling day, the controller takes a markdown in accordance with the tags attached to the sales checks. The next day the tags are removed, and the balance of the merchandise is available for selling immediately, requiring no price changing or new tickets.

Obviously, different levels of retailing will handle these problems in accordance with the needs of their operation as they see it. Indeed, different departments within a given store may use different price-ticket policies for the same reason.

[14] Re-Marking Procedures

Re-marking refers to the practice of replacing a price ticket on an item of merchandise with a new price ticket, or altering the existing retail price on a price ticket with a price change.

Re-marking may be necessary for the following reasons:

1. Stock-merchandise price tickets may be removed by customers or children, either accidentally or intentionally.

2. Stock-merchandise price tickets may become separated and lost from the merchandise as a result of the physical handling of the merchandise by stockpeople and others.

3. Customers may return merchandise with the price ticket removed. Such an item may have been received as a gift, or a customers may have removed the price ticket for some deceitful reason. (On a gift sale, some stores remove only the price portion of the price ticket so that such returns may be identified, and have available all of the necessary data to make re-marking easier.)

4. Stock-merchandise price tickets may become torn, damaged, soiled, or mutilated as a result of the constant handling by customers and sales personnel.

5. New price tickets may be necessary to conform to the store policy when price changes are taken, either upward or downward.

6. Customer purchases that are returned for refund, credit, or exchange may require new price tickets.

7. New price tickets may be required as a result of finding incorrectly printed tickets on items in stock.

8. Merchandise returned from the branches to the main store may need new price tickets because price changes were taken at the branch that do not conform to the main store prices.

9. Premarking refers to the practice of supplying a vendor with preprinted store tickets, and requesting him to attach the tickets to the merchandise before it is shipped to the store. Errors in the correct use of these tickets by the vendor, such as shipping merchandise to a store with the tickets of another retailer attached, necessitate new price tickets.

10. New price tickets are necessary to correct "ticket switching" practices on the part of customers, which result in a wrong price ticket on an item in stock.

11. New price tickets may be required on items used for window displays, interior displays, sketching, photographing, and fashion shows (in or out of the store). Many price tickets are removed from items under these circumstances.

12. Repairs returned to the store from vendors, and merchandise returned to the store from repair agencies, cleaners, tailors, etc., may require new price tickets.

It will be noted from the list of reasons stated that remarking involves two main types of merchandise: (1) those items that require a new price ticket and (2) those items that do not require a new price ticket but whose current price ticket does require some alteration.

Any procedures established to take care of these considerations that do not have as their main purposes discipline and control can result in actions detrimental to the best interests of the business. Obviously, an independent merchant can resort to any re-marking procedure, since he is responsible only to himself for his own actions. But organizations that employ personnel to conduct the affairs of the business must establish rules, regulations, and procedures with regard to re-marking. And management must insist upon strict adherence to the established procedures if organizational discipline is to be achieved.

Why are procedures, control, and discipline required?

1. The temptations of price manipulations and counting irregularities would be appealing to those who feel the need to resort to devious practices.

2. Price reductions for personal gain would be available to resourceful sales personnel.

3. An exaggerated shortage or overage could possibly result from a deliberate disrespect for established regulations and procedures.

4. The performance of the operation would be difficult, if not impossible, to evaluate and appraise.

5. All store rules, regulations, and procedures would be affected, and their breakdown would result in confusion and chaos as well as lack of respect for order and loyalty.

6. The customer image of the store could be severely damaged because of the existence in stock of the same item of merchandise at different retail prices. The procedures, control, and discipline would ensure that all re-marking operations throughout the store would be uniform.

Efficient and well-managed stores with an understanding of the need for control of price changes generally centralize the re-marking responsibility in the marking division under the supervision of the receiving or marking manager. Upon the proper authorized request, only a member of the marking division would be permitted to change the price on an existing price ticket, to remove an existing price ticket for the purpose of replacing it with a new one, or to attach a new price ticket to an item of merchandise that does not have one. The establishment of certain rules to strengthen the responsibility of the marking division are necessary, and can be stated as follows:

1. No store personnel may maintain a marking machine, marking equipment, or a marking pencil without the specific authorization of the marking manager.

2. No store personnel may maintain any blank price tickets without the specific authorization of the marking manager.

3. No marking or re-marking activity may be undertaken by any store personnel not authorized by the marking manager.

4. No marking or re-marking may be attempted with any makeshift writing device or writing implement without authorization from the marking manager.

5. No deviation from the prescribed marking procedures, or from the established price ticket presentation policies, may be attempted by any store personnel without the authorization of the marking manager.

6. An item in stock without a price ticket may not be sold, even though the retail price can be verified, unless and until a proper price ticket can be attached to the item.

7. All items of merchandise found in stock with a soiled, damaged, torn, mutilated price ticket, or with no price ticket, are to be removed from stock, and are not to be sold unless and until a new, proper price ticket can be attached to each item.

8. No marking representative may permit any personnel not assigned to the marking division to assist in the re-marking procedure without the specific authorization of the marking manager.

9. No representative of the marking division assigned to a re-marking task may relinquish control of, lend, or leave unattended any piece of marking equipment, writing implement, or price tickets without the authorization of the marking manager.

10. All price tickets, special re-marking pencils, and re-marking equipment must be kept under lock and key in a manner prescribed by the marking manager.

There may always be a good reason for making an exception to any of these established rules, but the exception should be authorized only by the marking manager and not by the merchandise manager or buyer without prior discussion with the marking manager.

Admittedly, a serious problem exists with the implementation of these rules, regulations, and procedures at the branch stores (especially the smaller ones), where the position of marking manager does not exist and where the remarking is the responsibility of the group or department manager. Admittedly, too, supervision of the re-marking procedure at the branches is at best a hit-or-miss effort. In many instances the selling activity continues while the re-marking is in progress, and the re-marking may be handled by a part-time salesperson with instructions from the group or department manager. While great stress is placed on the implementation of these procedures at the main store, there seems to be a complete lack of regard for these same procedures at the branch store. Justification for this difference in attitude between the main store and the branch store is that the stress at the branches is generally on payroll savings and not on procedures.

When a new price ticket is needed on an item for a reason that does not include a price change, then a re-marking authorization form is completed, in duplicate, by a salesperson or a stockperson but verified and authorized by the buyer, assistant buyer, or sales manager. One copy is attached to the item, for identification by the marking representative, and one copy is given to the marking division, which acts as an authorization to print the new price ticket and to attach the ticket to the item. When the new ticket has been attached to the item, the marking representative returns both copies of the re-marking authorization to the marking manager. Certain considerations of this activity should be followed:

1. The re-marking authorization should be completed in ink, not in pencil.

2. The old season letter or number should be placed on the new ticket, not the letter or number for the season in which the new price ticket is requested. In this way, the proper age of the item can be determined.

3. If the new price ticket is to be marked pursuant to the Federal Trade Commission Labeling Law, then the re-marking authorization should state the fiber content, country of origin, or any additional information required to satisfy the law.

4. The items to be reticketed should be placed in an area away from the selling floor for the performance of the task without interruption.

5. If more than one item is to be reticketed from the same re-marking authorization form, the marking representative must verify both the count and the fact that all of the items are identical.

6. Any remaining unused new price tickets must be returned to the marking manager.

The systems procedure of one store for the use of the re-marking authorization is as follows:

RE-MARKING AUTHORIZATION

Use: To reticket merchandise.
            To notify unit control of a credit (when necessary).

Requisition: Supply department

Procedure: Circle "credit" or "re-mark."
            Indicate type of ticket by checking "print" or "punch."
            Fill in:
            • Department number
            • Class code
            • Style number
            • Vendor number
            • Color code
            • Selling price
            Indicate any special information required, e.g., fiber identification.
            Retain "stub," top section, until merchandise is re-marked.
            Forward lower portion with merchandise to re-marking area. Marker forwards information to unit control (when necessary).

When an item requires a new price ticket because of a price change, the buyer completes a price-change form with all of the necessary information as indicated. His signature and that of his merchandise manager is required before the marking manager can act upon the request. The department has the responsibility of preparing the merchandise for the re-marking operation as follows:

1. Removing the merchandise to be re-marked from the selling area, or setting it aside on the selling floor.
2. Arranging the merchandise so it can be easily identified.
3. Sorting the merchandise according to style, color, size, and price for easy handling by the marker.
4. Not permitting the merchandise to be handled by department personnel while the re-marking is in progress.

The marker has the responsibility for the following:

1. Identifying the items to be re-marked.
2. Comparing the information on the existing price tickets with the information on the price-change form.
3. Counting the actual number of units to be re-marked and comparing the count with the number of units to be re-marked as stated on the price-change form.
4. Performing the marking function.
5. Collecting all of the removed price tickets.
6. Listing the actual number of units re-marked (verified quantity) on the price-change form.
7. Reviewing with the buyer or assistant any corrections in the price-change form as submitted by the department.

8. Obtaining the signature of the buyer or assistant on the completed price-change form to indicate that the department has verified the correction.

9. Signing the price-change form where indicated.

10. Returning the completed price-change form and the removed price tickets to the marking manager.

11. If the price change is made on the existing price tickets, returning only the completed price-change form to the marking manager.

The marking manager, after examination of the completed price-change form, will transfer it to the controller's office.

The systems write-up for one store describing the procedure for price-change authorization is herein stated:

PRICE-CHANGE AUTHORIZATION

Use: To mark up (raise) or mark down (lower) the selling price of merchandise.

Requisition (upon presentation of completed book):

New York: statistical department

Suburban store: controller's representative

Procedure: Check (x) the type of price change, "markdown" or "markup."

Enter the store name, department, number, and date.

Fill in:

● Vendor number

● Merchandise description

● Original count

Enter under "Unit Retail":

● "Old," previous price

● "New," markdown or markup price

Enter under "Price Change":
- "Unit," price change per unit
- "Total," total price change for item(s)

Fill in season code, reason (see numbered reasons at bottom of form), merchandise classification.

Enter any special instructions.

Add "Price Change Total" column and make entry under "Memo."

Enter markup month to date and markdown month to date under "Memo Total" and "Memo Cost" if requested by divisional merchandise manager.

Obtain buyer's and merchandise manager's signatures (or suburban store manager).

Send white (original) with merchandise to re-marking area:
- Marker signs under "Re-marked by" and enters actual count
- Forwards white copy to statistical department

Send yellow copy to divisional merchandise manager's office, where:
- Entry is made under department record
- Copy is returned to department

Retain pink copy in book for department record.

Several elements of the price-change procedure should be noted:

1. The form provides for a copy of the price-change form to be retained by the department.

2. If the price change is a markdown cancellation or a markup cancellation, the number of the original markdown or markup is required.

3. A store whose branches are making the same price change on merchandise in stock is to prepare the price-

change form so that carbon copies are automatically made for distribution to each branch.

4. Provision is made on the price-change form for the group manager's signature at the branch store. In most cases the group manager is also the verifier of his own price-change activity.

It should be noted here that three serious communication problems exist between the main store and the branch stores with regard to the price changes and the price-change form completed by the buyer.

1. The branch store may not have received the written notice of the price change. Buyer follow-up is essential to verify the receipt of the information. Although the mail between stores is usually made in a locked mail bag, important pieces of paper do go astray.

2. Not all main store buyers or store controllers make an effort to determine if the branch store has satisfactorily complied with the price change instructions received through the mail or over the teletype.

3. Not all price changes to be taken by the branches are recorded on a price-change form by the main-store buyer. Many of the price changes to be taken by the branch store are dictated over the telephone by the buyer or assistant. Misunderstood numbers, interruptions by customers and salespeople, sudden emergencies, and recording of the information on scrap paper (which can and does easily disappear) present a difficult situation. Failure to take these price changes at the branches as intended is one of the main reasons for different retail prices for the same item at the main store and at the branch stores.

The systems write-up for one store describing the procedure for notifying suburban stores of price changes is herein stated:

Use: To notify suburban stores of price changes.
Requisition: Supply department
Procedure (*initiated by New York department*):
                       Check type of price change in appropriate box.
                       Enter department date and date effective.
                       Fill in:
                       ● Vendor name, number
                       ● Style number
                       ● Merchandise
                       ● Old and new price
                       Write across sheet reason for price change.
                       Obtain signature of buyer and merchandise manager.
                       Retain original.
                       Forward via house mail to each suburban store, as indicated.
Group Manager: Fill out a "Price-Change Authorization" to take price change (markup or markdown).
                       Indicate "Price-Change Authorization" book and check number in space provided on "Price-Change Bulletin."
                       Fill in quantity under "Actual Quantity" on "Price-Change Bulletin."
                       Sign and return to buyer in New York with yellow copy of "Price-Change Authorization."

It should be realized that a record of all price changes, main store or branches, is necessary in order to determine the value of the merchandise on hand, the extent of the shortages, and the resultant gross margin.

Generally, priorities are established for the order in which price-change requests should be handled. While all price-change requests are important, fashion items receive prior consideration because of the very nature of the merchandise. Buyers, however, are expected to present their price-change request within a reasonable number of days before the price change is needed.

We have noted that the time, effort, personnel, supplies, handling, and paperwork required in the completion of a price change is more expensive than the original pricing of the merchandise. For this reason, some stores overlook the accuracy and control of a price change in favor of a less costly but less disciplined procedure.

[15] Special Problems

Revision of Retail Downward

Revision of retail downward may be the result of any one of several factors. It may be a cancellation of an additional mark-up after the buyer finds that he must reduce the additional markup in part or entirely because the merchandise would not sell at his over-optimistically increased price. On the other hand, it may be a reduction (or correction) of an originally high retail price caused by the buyer's unwarranted enthusiasm. In either case, a revision of retail downward may be taken only when it will *not* reflect a depreciation in cost value of the merchandise, and it must be authorized by the controller.

A revision of retail downward may be necessary to correct a mechanical mistake in original pricing. Or, a vendor may allow a rebate or cumulative quantity discount in the cost price of goods already in the store's stock, in which case the buyer may revise the retail price downward *in proportion* to the reduction in cost.[1]

---

[1] Bernard P. Corbman and Murray Krieger, *Mathematics of Retail Merchandising, Theory and Practice* (2nd ed., New York: Ronald Press, 1970), p. 93.

1. Markdown Cancellations. After merchandise has been reduced it may be necessary to restore the price of the item to its original price or to some price higher than the reduced one. Although the increase represents an upward revision, it is treated as a cancellation of all or a part of the markdown.

2. Markup Cancellations. When the retail price of an item is increased with the understanding that it will be lowered at some future time, an additional markup is taken for the increase in price and a markup cancellation is used to reduce the price. Technically it should be considered a markdown, but, in view of the circumstances, a cancellation is taken. A markup cancellation is also taken to correct an error in re-marking. Similar to the consideration applied to markdown cancellations, only the purchases of the current season may receive a markup cancellation. In some retail operations, markdowns are permitted to cancel an additional markup.

3. Rebates from Vendors. Retail stores receive a rebate or allowance from vendors for several reasons, among them quantity purchases resulting in a quantity discount, or an allowance to compensate the retailer for his stock on hand in a falling wholesale market.

Some rebates require that the retailer reduce the retail prices of the current inventory. When the retail prices are reduced, the retail value of the inventory is also reduced. However, these reductions are not markdowns but adjustments in the retail value of the purchases. A revision of retail downward is taken for the amount of the reduction. When the amount of the markdown is in excess of the retail equivalent of the allowance, the excess is treated as a markdown. To illustrate:

If the markdown is $1,500 and the rebate is $500 in a department operating with a 50-percent mark-on, the equivalent retail value of the rebate is $1,000. Therefore, $1,000 is considered a revision of the retail downward and $500 considered a markdown.

4. P.M.'s, Bonuses, Commissions. Salespeople's salaries consist of wages, commissions, P.M.'s, and the bonuses that are paid to regular and extra salespeople. All of these items are classified as selling expenses. Markdowns are not taken for any of these items.

5. Employee Discounts. The total company markdowns generally do not include discounts to employees. However, the markdowns of each selling department includes discounts granted to employees.

6. Manipulations. Buyers in difficulty are known to attempt to manipulate figures in an effort to hide an apparent shortage or to change certain inventory figures. For example, recording markdowns that do not exist or that are not actually taken will tend to reduce a shortage. Price reductions taken as markup cancellations instead of markdowns tend to reduce the amount of markdowns taken. Revisions of retail downward that are taken instead of markdowns tend to inflate the mark-on.

7. Trucking-Marking Agencies. Some stores make use of the services of an outside agency to mark or ticket the ready-to-wear. It is intended as a time- and expense-saving device. However, errors in pricing do result from this activity, necessitating the need for correction and revision. (See Appendix page 187.)

[Appendix A]
Forms

Introduction to Forms

The forms shown on the following pages are all mentioned in the text and are presented for reference purposes. They are representative of the many types of forms used in retail operations as part of the systems and procedures involving markdowns. Naturally, the nature of the operation will determine the kind of form that will best serve the purposes for which it is intended.

INVENTORY REQUEST
PREPARE A SEPARATE FORM FOR EACH DEPARTMENT

STORE NO._____ DEPT. NO._____ DATE_____

IS THIS CONTROLLED MERCHANDISE ?   YES ☐   NO ☐
(FOR H. O. USE ONLY)

ATTENTION: STORE MANAGER

THIS INVENTORY MUST BE TAKEN AT THE CLOSE OF BUSINESS:_____

THE COMPLETED INVENTORY FORM MUST BE MAILED TO THE H. O. NO LATER THAN:_____

Mfr. No.	Style No.	Item No.	Unit Retail Price	ITEM (Coat, Dress, Etc.)	Color	Size	Units on the Selling Floor	Units in AD or Reserve Stock	TOTAL UNITS

APPROXIMATELY HOW MANY OF THE TOTAL UNITS HAVE IBM TICKETS ?_____

APPROXIMATELY HOW MANY OF THE TOTAL UNITS HAVE DENNISON PIN TICKETS ?_____

REMARKS:_____

_____

_____

MAKE SURE ALL INFORMATION IS FILLED IN BEFORE MAILING THIS FORM TO **H. O.**

STORE MANAGER :_____DATE:_____
SIGNATURE

A Request-for-Store-Inventory Form Used by a Chain Operation

MERCHANDISE TRANSFER

DO NOT LIST MORE THAN ONE DEPARTMENT ON THIS TRANSFER

FROM RE NUMBER	TO STORE NUMBER	MERCHANDISE TRANSFER NUMBER	DEPARTMENT NUMBER	DATE SHIPPED			TOTAL AMOUNT (FOR H.O. USE ONLY)
		No. 131059		MO.	DAY	YR.	$

:D TO:

SHIPPED VIA: _____

:S: _____

CARRIER RECEIPT NO. _____

ND STATE _____ ZIP CODE _____

IF SHIPPED VIA A CARRIER — ATTACH SIGNED
BILL OF LADING RECEIPT TO WHITE TRANSFER

COMPLETE ALL COLUMNS BELOW

FG. O.	STYLE NO.	ITEM NO.	DESCRIPTION OF ITEM	TOTAL SINGLE UNITS SHIPPED	UNIT RETAIL PRICE	

DO NOT WRITE
IN THIS AREA

RANSFER AUTHORIZATION # ➝ | No. |

SIGNED _____
MANAGER'S FULL NAME

A Merchandise-Transfer Form Used by a Chain Operation

PRICE CHANGE

PART 1   B

DEPT. NO.   CLASS   DATE

(X) TO SHOW TYPE

MARK-DOWN	
CANCELLATION OF MARK-DOWN	
MARK-UP	

ISSUED AT:
☐ STORE 1
☐ STORE 2
☐ STORE 3
☐ MAIN STORE
☐ WAREHOUSE

ISSUE SEPARATE SHEETS FOR MARK-DOWN, CANCELLATION, MARK-UP, STOLEN, AND SALVAGE ITEMS.

SHOW REASON BY LETTER	ORIGINAL MARK-DOWN NUMBER	Statis- tical	ITEM DESCRIPTION — VENDOR — STYLE — NAME	QUANTITY	SEA. LET.	VERIFIED QUANTITY	OLD RETAIL	NEW RETAIL	DIFFERENCE	AMOUNT
A. PROMOTIONAL PURCHASE REMAINDERS										
B. SLOW MOVING OR INACTIVE STOCK										
C. SPECIAL SALES FROM STOCK										
D. PRICE ADJUSTMENTS										
E. BROKEN ASSORTMENTS AND REMNANTS										
F. SHOPWORN, SOILED OR DAMAGED										
G. ALLOWANCE TO CUSTOMER										
H. STOLEN										
J. SALVAGE										

DO NOT ENTER ANY PRICE CHANGES BELOW THIS LINE

DEPT. MGR'S SIGNATURE	DATE	MDSE. V. P. OR MGR'S SIGNATURE	DATE	MARKER'S SIGNATURE	DATE

TOTAL — DO NOT CARRY THIS TOTAL FORWARD

FOR STATISTICAL DEPT USE ONLY

SEND PART 1 TO STATISTICAL; PART 2 TO NEW YORK STORE DEPT. MGR.; LEAVE PART 3 IN BOOK

A Price-Change Form

Shopping Calendar

Here's the pattern that stores generally follow in setting up promotions throughout the year. Some are sales, others are special promotions that sometimes, but not always, include a sale on merchandise being promoted. (Source: National Retail Merchants' Assn.)

JANUARY	FEBRUARY	MARCH	APRIL
White sales, store-wide clearance, resort wear, fur sales, furniture sales (3rd week)	Furniture and home furnishings sales, Valentine's Day, Washington's Birthday, housewares	Housewares, china, silver, garden supplies, spring and Easter promotions	Spring-cleaning supplies, moth preventives, paints, housewares, fur storage campaigns, outdoor furniture
MAY	JUNE	JULY	AUGUST
Mother's Day, summer sportswear, air-conditioning, fans, bridal business, garden supplies, outdoor furniture	Graduation, Father's Day, bridal gifts, sportswear, men's sportswear, men's camp clothes and supplies, vacation needs	July 4th clearances, sporting goods, sportswear, furniture sales (4th week)	Furniture sales, fur sales, back-to-school, fall fashions, fall fabrics
SEPTEMBER	OCTOBER	NOVEMBER	DECEMBER
Back-to-school, fall fashions, men's and boys' sportswear, home furnishings, china and glassware, accessories	Women's coats, suits and furs, men's and boys' outerwear, millinery and accessories, Columbus Day, home furnishings	Christmas toys, pre-Christmas value promotions, Thanksgiving weekend sales, china, glassware, table linens, home furnishings	Christmas campaign, gift promotions, resort wear—north and south (4th week)

A Promotional Calendar for Markdown Planning

167

STORE	DEPT.	PURCHASES	SALES	MARKDOWNS	%	INVENTORY
865	80	11,193.99	8,361.34	270.35	3.23	11,524.5
867	80	10,903.70	7,385.55	343.32	4.64	20,269.2
868	80	13,691.74	10,601.52	480.37	4.53	20,319.4
870	80	7,296.11	5,578.88	31.84	.57	18,571.7
873	80	4,453.70	4,523.47	229.68	5.07	10,440.9
875	80	6,974.34	4,729.28	130.67	2.76	17,098.3
878	80	6,285.07	7,456.46	340.14	4.56	21,945.3
880	80	6,817.34	5,614.99	218.72	3.89	10,813.5
887	80	6,995.11	5,661.92	191.53	3.38	11,596.8
888	80	7,120.13	6,065.22	409.08	6.74	16,066.7
890	80	7,391.03	8,199.22	591.08	7.20	19,228.8
891	80	7,511.78	5,853.55	132.26	2.25	10,740.7
898	80	878.58	1,157.03	93.48	8.07	7,659.1
899	80	79,527.37-				33,275.5
990	80	1,911.22-				8,065.4
993	80					
995	80					43,667.9
997	80					
998	80	773.60				9,928.4
999	80	112,180.35-		4,919.79		287,141.9
DEPARTMENT TOTALS						
	80	1,936,726.53	1,631,709.71	78,673.87	4.82	4,873,746.7

A Computer Printout, Indicating Dollar and Percentage Markdowns and Open-to-Buy Position, Used in a Multi-Unit Opertion

168

SLOW-SELLING STOCK

Inventory Date _____   Dept. _____

These sheets must be turned into the merchandise office on the 15th of
each month with all data shown complete.

Ref. Number	ARTICLE	Season Letters	INVENTORY							
			Date		Date		Date		Date	
			Quan.	Price	Quan.	Price	Quan.	Price	Quan.	Price

A Prior Report Form

MARKDOWN SHEET

YOUR STORE NO.	DATE	MARKDOWN SHEET NO.	DEPT. NO. LIST ONE ONLY	AMOUNT HOME OFFICE USE ONLY
		№ 257731		

LIST AUTHOR-IZATION NO.	DEPT. NO.	S	MFG. NO.	STYLE NO.	ITEM NO.	ITEM (DRESS COAT BLOUSES)	UNIT (Single Piece) PRICE		DIFFERENCE IN UNIT PRICE	TOT SIN UN MAR DO
							FROM	TO		
COL. 1	COL. 2	COL. 3	COL 4	COL. 5	COL. 6	COL. 7	These Numbers Must Be Filled In At All T			
		↑	THESE NUMBERS MUST BE FILLED IN COMPLETELY		↑					

↑ ↑ **THE MARKDOWN AUTHORIZATION NUMBER MUST BE LISTED.**

Reason for this Markdown_____ ◄IMPORTAN
(DAMAGE-PROMOTIONAL ETC.) ◄IMPORTAN
◄MUST B
This Markdown Authorized by_____ ◄FILLED I
(LIST FULL NAME ABOVE)

INSTRUCTIONS

1. **DO NOT LIST MARKDOWNS IN THIS BOOK IF AUTHORIZATION FOR MARKDOWN IS RECEIVED IN THE STORE BY I. B. M. SHEETS OR DUPLICATING SHEETS.**
2. Mail White (Original) Copy of this Markdown Sheet in **PINK INVENTORY CONTROL ENVELOPE**

A Markdown Form Used by a Multi-Unit Operation

pt. No. _____ Department _____

source Name _____ Address _____

source No. _____ Type of Mdse. _____

onth	$ Retail Purchases	$ Vendor Returns	$ Mark-down	$ Net Sales	% Initial Markon	% Maintained Markon
nuary						
bruary						
March						
April						
May						
June						
July						
gust						
tember						
ctober						
ember						
ember						

ments _____

A Vendor Analysis Form

MARKDOWN ANALYSIS

Dept. No. ————————————————— Dept. Name _____

Month of ———————————————— Resource _____

Style No.	No. of Items	$ Original Retail	First M.D. Price	$ Net Ret. Sales	$ Total M.D.	%M.D.	Reason

Reason Nos:

1. Competition

2. Shopworn

3. Salvage and Breakage

4. Broken Assortments and Remnants

5. Customer Allowance

6. Unseasonable

7. Slow-selling

8. Fabric and Quality

9. Style, Color, Size

10. Special Sales

11. Other

A Markdown Analysis Form

172

MONTHLY AGE ANALYSIS FOR _____

Dept. Name and No. _____

Store	Months 0 - 7 $	%	Months 8 - 13 $	%	Months Over 13 $	%	Date of Inventory

An Age Analysis Form

173

LOAN RECEIPT

N? 619

MERCHANDISE REQUISITIONED FROM DEPT. # _____

DATE _____ 197__ BY _____ DEPT. _____

Quantity	Mfg.	Style No.	Size	Color	TYPE OF ITEM	Unit	Retail

Location of Merchandise Requisitioned _____

Name and Number of Borrower _____

Merchandise Returned to Stock _____

Signature of Recipient

The merchandise borrowed on this receipt must be returned within 30 days or a renewal arrangement made with the buyer and a new receipt issued.

A Loan Receipt Form

CANCELLATION NOTICE

DATE_____197___

Gentlemen:

Referring to our Order No._____confirmed on_____

and due on_____we advise you herewith that the same has been canceled.

Reason_____

_____ Dept._____ Amount $_____

Buyer's Signature_____ Mdse. Mgr. Signature_____

A Cancellation or an Open-Order Form

175

AUTHORIZATION FOR SALVAGE MARK DOWN SHEET

DATE EFFECTIVE | DEPARTMENT NO. | FILL IN SERIAL NUMBER OF MARK DOWN SHEETS

VENDOR NO.	MERCHANDISE	ORIG. COUNT	REMARK COUNT	UNIT RETAIL		PRICE CHANGE		SEASON CODE	* REASON	MDSE. CLASS
				OLD	NEW	UNIT	TOTAL			

MEMO TOTAL	MEMO	MEMO COST
MARK-UP MO. TO DATE	TOTAL	MARKDOWN MO. TO DATE

INSTRUCTIONS:

BUYER - FILL OUT ABOVE FORM AND SECURE MDSE. MGR'S SIGNATURE ON BOTH AUTHORIZATION AND MARKDOWN SHEET. SEND AUTHORIZATION AND ORIGINAL OF MARKDOWN SHEET TO THE MARKING ROOM.

RECEIVING DEPT. - AFTER AUTHORIZATION SHEET HAS BEEN CHECKED AND STAMPED BY THE RECEIVING DEPT. IT MUST BE SENT TO THE SUPPLY DEPT. WITH THE MERCHANDISE TO BE SALVAGED.

A Salvage Form

176

ON ORDER REPORT

(TO NEAREST THOUSAND DOLLARS)

WEEK ENDING _____

EPT.	SEASON 1				SEASON 2				SEASON 3			
	Domestic		Foreign		Domestic		Foreign		Domestic		Foreign	
	Retail	%	Retail	%	Retail	%	Retail	%	Retail	%	Retail	%
O												
0												
O												
O												
O												
O												
O												
O												
AL LL TS.												
O												
2												
4												
6												
7												
TAL SES												
4												
5												
TAL TS TS												
4												
5												
6												
8												
AL RIE												
3												
2												
AL SES TERS												

A Weekly Open-Order Form

177

CONTENTS: MERCHANDISE RETURN REQUESTED

DM 105136

ACCOUNTS PAYABLE STUB

CHARGE TO		
NAME		STORE NAME
ADDRESS		
TOWN	STATE	DEPT.

SEND TO		
NAME		STORE
ADDRESS		
TOWN	STATE	**DM 105136**

MERCHANDISE SHIPPED BY AGREEMENT OF	YOUR MR.	OUR MR.

QUANTITY	DESCRIPTION OF MERCHANDISE	UNIT COST	TOTAL COST

REASON FOR RETURN		MDSE. COST	
	VALUE OF CUSTOMER MDSE.	IN ☐ OUT ☐ TRANSPORTATION	
DATE	TERMS	TOTAL COST	

STORE NAME

YOU WILL RECEIVE
AN ORIGINAL INVOICE

★ RETURN CUSTOMER OR STOCK REPAIRS TO:	ISSUED BY STORE	DEPT.

CREDIT	★ STOCK REPAIR	★ CUSTOMER REPAIR	**DM 105136**
Please send us a credit memo. If no amount is due you, please send us your check.	Please send us a credit memo. Bill us for the exact cost as shown when the merchandise is returned to us.	Sent to you for repair per instructions. Value of goods will be charged to you if merchandise is not returned in ____ days.	**ATTENTION VENDOR:** REFER TO THIS NO. ON ANY COMMUNICATION REGARDING THIS SHIPMENT. ON EXCHANGES OR REPAIRS PLEASE PRINT THIS CLAIM NUMBER ON YOUR INVOICE WHICH ACCOMPANIES RETURN OF OUR MERCHANDISE.

REFER TO YOUR INVOICE NUMBER:

BUYER'S SIGNATURE	MDSE MGR'S. SIGNATURE	GEN. MDSE. MGR. (OVER $1,000 AT COST) SIGNATURE

A Return-to-Vendor Form

WEEKLY SALES REPORT

Week Ending_____

	Quantity of Items Sold	Total Retail
Rugs & Remnants		
Sofas		
Chairs (upholstered)		
Sofa Beds		
Occasional Tables		
Occasional Pieces		
Modular B/R Pieces		
Dining Rooms		
Bedrooms		
Bedding (Pieces)		
Dining Room Tables		
Dining Chairs		
Lamps		
Desks		
Mirrors		
Beds & Headboards		
Summer Furniture		
Imports		
Total Dollar Volume (approx)		

Name_____

Sales Hours_____

Store_____

A Divisional Weekly Sales Form

179

STYLE SELLING SHEET

DPD REPORT # | DEPT 32 | PAGE NO 5 | WEEK ENDING MO 09 DAY 21

CLASS	AOR	COST	RETAIL	STYLE	T/Y/P/E	PR CAT	VENDOR NAME	VENDOR NO	MKDN MO	DAY	CHAIN TOTAL SALES TO DATE	CHAIN SALES THIS WEEK	CHAIN END OF WEEK STOCK	CHAIN DATE FIRST SHPMT (MO DAY)	CHAIN DATE LATEST SHPMT (MO DAY)	CHAIN QTY LATEST SHPMT	NY TOTAL SALES TO DATE	NY SALES THIS WEEK	NY END OF WEEK STOCK	NY DATE LATEST SHPMT (MO DAY)	NY QTY LATEST SHPMT	STYLE DESCRIPTION	WAREHOUSE	ON ORDER
01	01	22.25	46.00	6497	0	2	ALDANA	945					08 19						4	08 19		SNAPPA RECT WITH FLAP		
							RETAIL TOTAL																	
04	01	40.50	50.00	3406	0	2	STA ALIGAT	084			4	1	21	08 05	09 02	25	3	1	4	08 05	4	4GEN ALLIG EAST WEST		
04	01	30.50	50.00	3660	0	2	STERLING	084			8	2	40	08 05	09 16	7	3	1	5	08 05	1	4GEN ALLIG DIH POUCH		
							RETAIL TOTAL					3	41						5					
03	01	30.50	55.00	3661	0	2	STERLING	084			3	1	22	08 12	09 16	5	1		3	08 12		4GEN ALLIG CLASS POUC		
03	01	30.50	55.00	3662	0	2	STERLING	084			3		24	09 02	09 16	12			7	08 12		ALLIG PANEL POUCH		
03	01	30.50	55.00	3681	0	2	STERLING	084			3	1	24	08 12	09 16	9	3		3	08 12		4GEN ALLIG SATCHEL		
03	01	30.50	55.00	3682	0	2	STERLING	084			5		08 05	08 05					7	08 05		4ALLIGATOR		
							RETAIL TOTAL				4	2	70											
03	01	36.50	65.00	3812	0	2	STERLING	084			2	1	20	08 05	09 16	13	1		3	08 05		4GEN ALLIG PUSH LOCK	1	
03	01	36.50	65.00	3813	0	2	STERLING	084			2	1	22	08 05	09 02	24	1		4	08 05		4GEN ALLIG INLAY POU		1
03	01	36.50	65.00	4231	0	2	GEN ALIGAT	084					26	08 05	09 16	8			4	08 12		2OR SATCHEL	2	
03	01	36.50	65.00	4263	0	2	GEN ALLIG	084			2		27	08 05	09 16	11	1		3	08 05		4ENVELUPE		
03	01	36.50	65.00	4684	0	2	STERLING	084			7	3	117	08 05	09 02	25	2	2	18	08 05		4GENALLIG LGE POUCH		
							RETAIL TOTAL																	
03	01	39.16	70.00	2984	0	2	AU SAC MOD	990					09 02						3	09 02		3CALF		
03	01	38.17	70.00	2990	0	2	AU SAC MOD	990					09 02						3	09 02		3CALF		
03	01	39.16	70.00	3029	0	2	AU SAC MOD	990					09 02						3	09 02		3CALF		
03	01	36.50	70.00	4691	0	2	STERLING	084			1		24	08 05	09 16	5	1		3	08 05		4GEN ALIG CLASIC POU		
03	01	36.50	70.00	5004	0	2	STERLING	084					28	08 05	09 16	26	1		3	08 05		4GEN ALING DIH POUCH		
03	01	36.50	70.00	5005	0	2	STERLING	084			2	2	24	08 05	09 16	21	1		1	08 05		4GEN ALLIG LGE SATCH		
							RETAIL TOTAL				3		76					5		10					
							CLASS TOTAL				1659	260	4525					660	114	611					
11	11	3.25	6.00	716	0	2	BONITA	026			216	7	119	06 10	09 23	72	32	2	16	09 23		10SMALL BARREL SHOULDR	72	6
11	11	3.25	6.00	1335	0	2	LETISS	006			163	11	111	07 08	09 23	60	19		17	09 23		12SMALL SUEDE CHAIN CH		
11	11	2.89	6.18	1474	0	2	RUZE	018					09 02				2			09 02		2SHAG CHN BARREL		
11	11	2.85	6.18	1474	1	2	RUZE	018					09 02				4			09 02		4SAME AS STYLE 1474		
11	11	3.25	6.00	3915	0	2	JINDSS	658			183	34	161	07 15	09 16	144	22		26	09 23		4GRAIN RING SHOUSE		
11	11	3.25	6.00	7332	0	2	LETISSE	006			99		45	06 10	07 15	130	14	1	5	07 01		12SMALL DBL HUL POUCH		
11	11	3.25	6.00	7335	0	2	LETISSE	006			140	2	100	07 08	09 23	60	18	1	30	09 23		24SMALL SUEDE CHAIN CH		
11	11	3.25	6.00	7338	0	2	LETISSE	006			122	18	118	07 08	09 23	96	18	2	12	09 23		12SUEDE XIP SOFT POUCH		
11	11	3.25	6.00	7340	0	2	LETISSE	006			111	6	69	08 26	08 19	180	17		7	08 26		24SML SUEDE S S POUCH		24
							RETAIL TOTAL				1034	82	703					140	11	112					
11	11	3.15	7.00	624	0	2	LETISSE	006			248	20	76	06 10	09 16	30	24		6	06 10		24GRAIN SHOULDER VAGAB		24
11	11	3.15	7.00	808	0	2	BONITA	026			219	3	49	06 10	09 23	24	24	3	34	09 23		3BSMALL GRAIN LUK SHL		126 30

180

	MO	DAY	YR.

DEPT.	CLASS	PRICE	HOUSE	STYLE	COLOR	SIZE	STORE 1 SALE UNITS	STORE 1 RETURN UNITS	STORE 2 SALE UNITS	STORE 2 RETURN UNITS	STORE 3 SALE UNITS	STORE 3 RETURN UNITS	STORE 4 SALE UNITS	STORE 4 RETURN UNITS	STORE 5 SALE UNITS	STORE 5 RETURN UNITS	NET UNITS	NET DOLLARS
374	17	1300	010	6789									3		1			
374	17	1200	010	4760									6		1			
374	17	1000	010	4781														
374	17	1300	010	4740														
374	17	1000	016	1414					1									
374	17	1200	016	1814					2				2 8		9			
374	17	1300	018	6553					1 1									
374	17	1000	018	6658					1 9		1 7							

374	19	1000	265	5213							1		1					
374	17	800	766	5150					4		1		1 2		2 4			
374	11	1000	766	6637					2		1				1			
374	18	1800	790	6302					6 3		2							
374	13	1900	104	9117					1		5 3		1		1			

374	23	400	004	9000							1 1		2					
374	23	400	419	9000							1 1				1			
374	23	400	007	9000					1		1 2		4		1			
374	23	400	112	3137					2 1						2 4 1			
374	23	400	112	1425					1 1									
374	23	400	112	1011					6									
374	23	400	115	3114					3 1				1		1			
374	23	400	115	1016					1						1			
374	23	400	143	3600					2 2		1 2		2					
374	23	1900	996	3344					2 3				4					
374	23	400	996	6653									1					
374	23	400	996	6773									1					
374	23	500	996	8816					1									
374	23	400	996	8856					3				2					
374	23	400	996	8864					1		1		3 1 1		1 3 1			
374	23	400	996	8889							2 3		1 1		1 1			
374	23	600	996	9197							3				1 1			
374	23	800	996	9287							1		1		1 2			
374	23	400	996	9288					1									
374	23	400	996	9433					5 1									
374	23	500	961	9466					9 1		2 3		1		9 1			
374	23	800	961	3065					5 2		3				5 2			
374	23	600	966	6530					4 5		1				2 0			
374	23	400	961	5170														

| 374 | 35 | 2000 | 104 | 453168 | | | | | 4 5 | | 2 3 1 | | 1 3 | | 2 0 | | G | |

ADVERTISED MARKDOWN AUTHORIZATION

TO BE USED FOR ADVERTISING MARKDOWNS ONLY
THIS IS YOUR MARKDOWN SHEET, DO NOT ENTER
IN YOUR MARKDOWN BOOK

AD DATE_____

INSTRUCTIONS:

1. The Store must fill in all shaded areas below:
   A. Quantity on Hand Prior to AD
      (If none on hand prior to AD, enter none in this column
      and enter item substituted under AD Change)
   B. Stroke count of units sold during AD (ᵀᴴᴴᴸ)
   C. Total Number of Units Sold at the end of the AD period

2. AD Changes — If AD is changed at local level fill in all
   columns in the AD change area and indicate the name of person authorizing this change.

3. Distribution: Upon completion of AD — Mail
   A. White Copy in the Pink Inventory Control Envelope to the Home Office
   B. Blue Copy with tear sheet of AD to Home Office
   C. Retain Yellow Copy as your Store File Copy for future reference

4. This AD was run in (Insert name of newspaper)_____

Use your store stamp here ON ALL 3 COPIES

| | NEWSPAPER | NEWSPAPER | MAILER |

MFG. #	STYLE #	ITEM #	ON HAND PRIOR TO AD	DESCRIPTION	REG. PRICE	ADV PRICE	DIFF	USE SPACE BELOW FOR (ᵀᴴᴴᴸ) COUNT	TOTAL NO. OF UNITS SOLD

AD CHANGE Authorized By

STORE NO.	AD DATE	DEPT.NO.	HOME OFFICE USE ONLY	AUTHORIZATION NO.	DATE SUBMITTED	STORE MGR'S SIGNATURE

USE AD DISTRIBUTION FOR DISTRIBUTION TO STORES   INSTRUCTIONS TO N.Y. — RECODE ALL AD CHANGES

UPON COMPLETION OF AD, MERCHANDISE IS TO RETURN TO ORIGINAL PRICE

A Markdown Form for Advertised Items Used by a Multi-Unit Store

CHECK TYPE OF PRICE CHANGE BELOW				**PRICE CHANGE**	9854

MARK DOWN	CANCELLATION		MARK UP	**BULLETIN**	
	MARK DOWN	MARK UP			

DEPT.	DATE	DATE EFFECTIVE	PRICE CHANGE BK-CHK NO.	**NEW YORK**

VENDOR NAME-NUMBER	STYLE	MERCHANDISE	OLD PRICE		NEW PRICE		ACTUAL QUAN.

BUYER'S SIGNATURE   DATE   MDSE. MGR'S SIGNATURE   DATE   GROUP MGR'S SIGNATURE   DATE

A Price-Change Form

183

For re-pricing without re-ticketing, the Dennison Re-marker is available in two basic types. One type cancels the old price and simultaneously prints the new price; the other type cuts off the old price and simultaneously prints the new one. Both types re-mark Dial-Set tags, Pinning Machine tickets, and Print-Punch tickets. You can make as many as two mark-ups or mark-downs without re-ticketing.

Knob-set for faster, easier re-pricing. You simply dial in the new price with a turn of the setting knob. This sets the price in *all* of the printing units. An indicator shows exactly what you have dialed.

Rewards to retailers. Your new price is *printed*. It looks official . . . inspires customer confidence . . . is clearly legible . . . minimizes unauthorized price changes. You re-mark right on the salesroom floor. No need to move merchandise or increase the load in the marking room. You minimize loss of selling time so you get greater turnover.

cancel & re-mark

cut-off & re-mark

A Knob-Set Re-Marker

Courtesy of Dennison Manufacturing Company, N.Y.

Re-marking Authorization

Use when price ticket is missing

IMPORTANT:
- Verify information - Examine like merchandise.
- Prepare in ink. Write legibly.

Description			No. of Pcs.
Season	Dept. No.	Line No.	
Vendor No.	Style No.	Retail Price	
		Dollars	Cents
Authorized Signature			Date

A Re-Marking Authorization Form

MONARCH RE-PRICE MARKERS

DIAL-A-PRICER EASE OF OPERATION

You set the price simply by dialing it once — the Models 105 and 106 then print on two, three and four-part tags. The printing characters match the size and style of those printed by the Monarch Model 100 ready-to-wear machine.

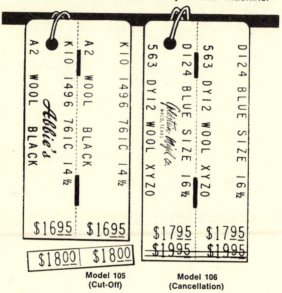

Model 105
(Cut-Off)

Model 106
(Cancellation)

MODEL 286 CANCELLATION RE-PRICE MARKER

The Model 286 is a Dial-a-Pricer Remarker for Model 86 Pin-On tickets. The 286 reprice-marks single or two-part Pin-On tickets with an index for setting the single or two-stop cycle to cancel both price lines on a two-part Monarch ticket.

Courtesy of Monarch Marking System Company, Dayton, Ohio

POSNER MARKING SERVICE PROBLEMS

STORE _____ REPORTED BY _____ DATE _____

DEPT.	DATE REC'D	VENDOR	POSNER APRON #	ORDER NO.	STYLE	#PCS. IN ERROR	DESCRIPTION OF ERROR	HOW MARKED	SHOULD BE

REPORT FULL DETAILS OF ERRORS: SPECIFY WHETHER DAMAGED, SOILED, OVER, SHORT, MARKED INCORRECTLY AS TO DEPARTMENT, SIZE, COLOR, STYLE OR RETAIL. IF INCORRECTLY RETAILED, SHOW WRONG RETAIL IN "HOW MARKED" COLUMN AND CORRECT RETAIL IN "SHOULD BE" COLUMN.

PREPARE IN TRIPLICATE. FORWARD TWO COPIES DAILY TO RECEIVING MANAGER, NEW YORK STORE, ONE COPY TO BUYER.

TRIPLICATE BUYER'S COPY

OFFICE USE ONLY

A Marking-Delivery Service Form

187

[Appendix B]
Glossary

Allowances to customers	The reductions in price allowed to customers because of some deficiency in or damage to the merchandise
As is	Used to describe the terms of sale to a customer for merchandise that is either damaged or irregular and that has been marked down
Breakage sheet	A sheet of paper, placed in a selling department, on which salespeople record items of merchandise completely destroyed or broken during a selling day.
Bulk marking	The procedure of recording the retail price of the item on the carton and then marking the individual item when it is sent to the selling floor.
Cost of markdown	The result obtained when the complement of the mark-on is applied to the retail value of the dollar markdown.
Cost or market, whichever is lower	The derived cost of the inventory after the markdowns have been taken. The derived cost is lower than the original cost and more nearly represents the market value of the merchandise.
Gross markdowns	The original amount of the markdowns taken.
Hash price	The mixture of merchandise from several price lines into one marked-down price.
Inventory or stock overage	The situation in which the physical inventory at retail is greater than the book inventory at retail.
Inventory or stock shortage	The situation in which the book inventory at retail is greater than the physical inventory at retail.

Leader	An item whose retail price has been reduced for the purpose of stimulating sales or attracting traffic.
Maintained mark-on	The difference between the initial mark-on and the cost value of the markdowns.
Markdown	A reduction in the retail price of an item (not including employees' discounts).
Markdown analysis	The recording of the reasons for markdowns taken during a certain period, for the purpose of analysis, evaluation, and appraisal, with a view to correction.
Markdown cancellation	An upward price adjustment of merchandise that was previously reduced.
Markdown control	A system to insure that every markdown taken is reported to the controller's office.
Markdown money	An amount given by a vendor to a retailer to enable the retailer to reduce an item of merchandise purchased from the vendor.
Markdown planning	The establishment of a dollar markdown or percentage markdown figure available for a given period of time.
Markdown percent	The relationship of the dollar markdown taken to the actual selling price expressed as a percentage.
Marker	An employee of the marking division.
Merchandise loan book	A book in which entries are made to record merchandise borrowed from a selling department by another department within the store.
Merchandise transfer	The movement of merchandise from one selling department to another selling department within the store or from store to store.
Monthly journal (markdowns)	A monthly departmental statement prepared by the controller's office that lists all markdowns and markdown cancellations.
Multiple pricing	Sometimes referred to as "twofers," the offering of two items for one price, as, "$5 Each, 2 for $9."
Net markdowns	The result of the subtraction of the markdown cancellations from the gross markdowns.

Nonmarking   Merchandise placed on sale without any form of price ticket or price identification. The price is usually stated on a sign at the point of purchase.

Open-to-reduce   The dollar amount of markdowns available to be taken during a given period.

Premarking   Marking done by the vendor at the request of the store. Price tickets are made out in the store and sent to the manufacturer to be attached to the merchandise.

Preretailing   The placing of the retail price of an item on the store's copy of a merchandise order in advance of the receipt of the merchandise.

Price change   The raising or lowering of the retail price of an item.

Price ticket   The ticket attached to the merchandise for the purpose of recording such needed information as season letter, retail price, style number, color, size, classification, and vendor.

Prior stock   Slow-selling goods, goods that have sold as rapidly as expected.

Promotional markdown The reduction of a retail price to satisfy the needs of a special sale or store-event sale.

Rebate   The refund of a part of the price paid by the store to a vendor, usually because of the large quantity of merchandise purchased.

Re-marking   The changing of a retail price either by issuing a new price ticket or by marking the new price on the existing price ticket.

Repair memo   The form used to record stock merchandise sent from a retail store to a vendor, cleaners, weavers, etc., for repair, cleaning, weaving, etc.

Retail deductions   The sum of the net sales, net markdowns, discounts to employees, and inventory shrinkage.

Retail reductions   The sum of the net markdowns, discounts to employees, and the inventory shrinkage.

Returns from customers	The items of merchandise puchased by customers from retail stores and returned by them for refund or credit.
Revision of retail downward	A procedure to correct an error in the original pricing of merchandise or to adjust the cost value of the current stock because of a rebate or a cumulative quantity discount.
Salvage merchandise	Items of merchandise that cannot be sold to customers or returned to vendors because of excessive damage.
Slow selling	Items that have been sold as rapidly as experience indicates that type of merchandise should.
Sweetening the stock	The purchasing of new merchandise to be mixed with existing stock to help the "old" merchandise sell without a markdown.
Ticket price	The recording of the retail price on the price ticket attached to an item of merchandise.
Vendor	A source of supply of merchandise for retail stores.
Vendor-marked or preticketed	Merchandise premarked by the vendor with the retail price.

Bibliography

Bell, Hermon F., and Muscarello, Louis C. *Retail Merchandise Accounting*. 3rd ed. New York: Ronald Press, 1961.

Davidson, William R., and Doody, Alton F. *Retailing Management*. 3rd ed. New York: Ronald Press, 1966.

Filene, Edward A. *The Model Stock Plan*. New York: McGraw-Hill, 1930.

Jones, Fred M. *Retail Merchandising*. Homewood, Ill.: Richard D. Irwin, Inc., 1957.

Krieger, Murray. *Decision-Making in Retailing and Marketing*. New York: Fairchild Publications, 1970.

———. *The Language of Retailing*. Professional Management Series. New York: LIM Press, 1969.

———. *Merchandising Math for Profit*. New York: Fairchild Publications, 1969.

———. *Merchandising Planbook and Sales Promotion Calendar*. New York: National Retail Merchants Association, 1969.

———. *Practical Problems in Retail Merchandising*. Professional Management Series. New York: LIM Press, 1969.

Krieger, Murray, and Corbman, Bernard P. *Mathematics of Retail Merchandising, Theory and Practice*. 2nd ed. New York: Ronald Press, 1970.

Wingate, John W., and Schaller, Elmer. *Techniques of Retailing*. 2nd ed. Englewood Cliffs, N.J.: Prentice-Hall, 1956.

Wingate, John W., Schaller, Elmer O., and Goldenthal, Irving. *Problems in Retail Merchandising*. 5th ed. Englewood Cliffs, N.J.: Prentice-Hall, 1961.

9757